50 Party Appetizer Recipes for Home

By: Kelly Johnson

Table of Contents

- Mini Caprese Skewers
- Spinach Artichoke Dip
- Bacon-Wrapped Dates
- Stuffed Mushrooms
- Bruschetta with Tomato and Basil
- Shrimp Cocktail
- Mini Quiches
- Deviled Eggs
- Chicken Satay Skewers
- Spanakopita (Greek Spinach Pie)
- Cheese Stuffed Jalapeños
- Crab Cakes
- Meatballs with BBQ Sauce
- Cucumber Bites with Herbed Cream Cheese
- Antipasto Skewers
- Smoked Salmon Canapés
- Buffalo Cauliflower Bites
- Baked Brie with Jam
- Mini Crab Salad Cups
- Spring Rolls with Dipping Sauce
- Gougeres (Cheese Puffs)
- Chicken Wings (Various Flavors)
- Avocado Shrimp Cups
- Stuffed Mini Peppers
- Prosciutto-Wrapped Melon
- Tomato Basil Bruschetta
- Asian Meatball Lettuce Wraps
- Mushroom Pate Crostini
- Mini Beef Empanadas
- Pigs in a Blanket
- Fried Ravioli with Marinara Sauce
- Teriyaki Chicken Skewers
- Bacon-Wrapped Jalapeño Poppers
- Tuna Tartare on Crispy Wontons
- Mini Reuben Sandwiches

- Spicy Thai Chicken Satay
- Crab Stuffed Avocado
- Mediterranean Phyllo Cups
- Bacon and Cheese Stuffed Mushrooms
- Artichoke Spinach Puff Pastry Pinwheels
- Caprese Salad Skewers
- Baked Buffalo Chicken Dip
- Chicken and Pineapple Skewers
- Greek Meatballs with Tzatziki Sauce
- Mini Lobster Rolls
- Sweet Potato Rounds with Goat Cheese
- Teriyaki Beef Skewers
- Caramelized Onion and Gruyere Tartlets
- Cajun Shrimp Cocktail
- Miniature Crab Cakes

Mini Caprese Skewers

Ingredients:

- Cherry or grape tomatoes
- Fresh mozzarella balls (bocconcini)
- Fresh basil leaves
- Balsamic glaze (optional)
- Salt and pepper, to taste
- Toothpicks or small skewers

Instructions:

1. Prepare Ingredients:
    - Rinse the cherry or grape tomatoes and pat them dry with paper towels.
    - Drain the fresh mozzarella balls (bocconcini) if they were stored in liquid, and pat them dry.
    - Wash and dry the fresh basil leaves.
2. Assemble Skewers:
    - Take a toothpick or a small skewer and thread on one cherry tomato.
    - Follow with a fresh basil leaf folded or rolled up.
    - Add a mozzarella ball (bocconcini) next.
    - Repeat this sequence until the skewer is filled, ending with a cherry tomato.
3. Season and Serve:
    - Arrange the assembled skewers on a serving platter.
    - Sprinkle with a pinch of salt and freshly ground black pepper, if desired.
    - Optionally, drizzle with balsamic glaze for added flavor and presentation.
4. Serve:
    - These Mini Caprese Skewers can be served immediately as a colorful and tasty appetizer for parties, gatherings, or any occasion.

Enjoy these bite-sized delights that capture the fresh and vibrant flavors of a traditional Caprese salad in a convenient, handheld format!

Spinach Artichoke Dip

Ingredients:

- 1 (10-ounce) package frozen chopped spinach, thawed and drained
- 1 (14-ounce) can artichoke hearts, drained and chopped
- 1 cup shredded mozzarella cheese
- 1/2 cup grated Parmesan cheese
- 1/2 cup sour cream
- 1/2 cup mayonnaise
- 1 clove garlic, minced
- 1/2 teaspoon salt
- 1/4 teaspoon black pepper

Instructions:

1. Preheat Oven: Preheat your oven to 350°F (175°C).
2. Prepare Ingredients: Thaw the frozen spinach according to package instructions and drain well, squeezing out excess water. Chop the artichoke hearts into smaller pieces if necessary.
3. Mix Ingredients: In a large mixing bowl, combine the chopped spinach, chopped artichoke hearts, shredded mozzarella cheese, grated Parmesan cheese, sour cream, mayonnaise, minced garlic, salt, and black pepper. Stir until well combined.
4. Bake: Transfer the mixture to a baking dish (8x8 inch or similar size) and spread it out evenly.
5. Bake: Bake in the preheated oven for about 25-30 minutes, or until the dip is bubbly and the top is lightly golden brown.
6. Serve: Remove from the oven and let it cool for a few minutes before serving. Serve warm with tortilla chips, crackers, sliced baguette, or vegetable sticks.
7. Enjoy: Enjoy this creamy Spinach Artichoke Dip as a delicious appetizer for parties or gatherings!

This recipe can be easily doubled for larger crowds, and you can customize it by adding a touch of cayenne pepper for a bit of heat or experimenting with different cheeses.

Bacon-Wrapped Dates

Ingredients:

- Medjool dates, pitted (about 12-16)
- Thinly sliced bacon, cut into halves or thirds (enough to wrap each date)
- Almonds or pecans, optional (1 for each date)
- Toothpicks or cocktail picks

Instructions:

1. Prepare Dates:
    - Preheat your oven to 375°F (190°C).
    - If your dates have pits, carefully slice each date lengthwise and remove the pit.
2. Stuff Dates (optional):
    - Optionally, you can stuff each date with an almond or pecan before wrapping them with bacon. This adds a crunchy texture and another layer of flavor.
3. Wrap with Bacon:
    - Take a piece of bacon and wrap it around each date. Secure the bacon in place by threading a toothpick or cocktail pick through the date.
4. Arrange on Baking Sheet:
    - Place the bacon-wrapped dates on a baking sheet lined with parchment paper or aluminum foil, with the seam side of the bacon facing down.
5. Bake:
    - Bake in the preheated oven for about 15-20 minutes, or until the bacon is crispy and cooked through. If you prefer crispier bacon, you can broil them for an additional 1-2 minutes, watching carefully to prevent burning.
6. Serve:
    - Remove from the oven and let them cool slightly before serving. Arrange on a platter and serve warm.
7. Enjoy:
    - Bacon-wrapped dates are delicious on their own or paired with a dipping sauce like balsamic glaze or a spicy aioli. They make a delightful appetizer for parties, gatherings, or as a special treat any time.

These bacon-wrapped dates are sure to be a hit with their irresistible combination of sweet, salty bacon and tender, caramelized dates.

Stuffed Mushrooms

Ingredients:

- 16-20 large button mushrooms
- 1/2 cup breadcrumbs (plain or seasoned)
- 1/2 cup grated Parmesan cheese
- 2-3 cloves garlic, minced
- 2 tablespoons fresh parsley, finely chopped
- 3 tablespoons olive oil
- Salt and pepper, to taste
- Optional: 1/4 cup chopped bacon or cooked sausage

Instructions:

1. Prepare the Mushrooms:
   - Preheat your oven to 375°F (190°C). Line a baking sheet with parchment paper or foil.
   - Clean the mushrooms with a damp cloth to remove any dirt. Remove the stems by gently twisting or cutting them off. Set the mushroom caps aside and finely chop the stems.
2. Prepare the Filling:
   - In a bowl, combine the chopped mushroom stems, breadcrumbs, grated Parmesan cheese, minced garlic, chopped parsley, olive oil, and salt and pepper to taste. Optionally, add chopped bacon or cooked sausage for extra flavor.
3. Stuff the Mushrooms:
   - Using a spoon or your hands, fill each mushroom cap generously with the breadcrumb mixture, pressing it down slightly to pack it in.
4. Bake:
   - Place the stuffed mushrooms on the prepared baking sheet. Bake in the preheated oven for about 20-25 minutes, or until the mushrooms are tender and the filling is golden brown and crispy on top.
5. Serve:
   - Remove from the oven and let cool slightly before serving. Arrange on a platter and garnish with additional chopped parsley if desired.
6. Enjoy:
   - Stuffed mushrooms can be served warm as a delicious appetizer for parties, gatherings, or as a tasty addition to any meal.

These stuffed mushrooms are versatile, and you can customize the filling by adding different herbs, cheeses, or proteins according to your preference. They are sure to be a crowd-pleaser at any occasion!

Bruschetta with Tomato and Basil

Ingredients:

- 4-6 ripe tomatoes, diced
- 1/4 cup fresh basil leaves, thinly sliced
- 2 cloves garlic, minced
- 1 tablespoon balsamic vinegar
- 3 tablespoons extra virgin olive oil
- Salt and pepper, to taste
- 1 French baguette or Italian bread, sliced
- Optional: Balsamic glaze for drizzling

Instructions:

1. Prepare the Tomato Basil Topping:
   - In a bowl, combine the diced tomatoes, thinly sliced fresh basil leaves, minced garlic, balsamic vinegar, extra virgin olive oil, salt, and pepper. Mix well to combine. Taste and adjust seasoning if needed. Set aside to marinate for at least 15-20 minutes to allow flavors to meld.
2. Prepare the Bread:
   - Preheat a grill pan or grill to medium-high heat. Alternatively, you can use a broiler in your oven.
   - Slice the French baguette or Italian bread into 1/2-inch thick slices. Brush each slice lightly with olive oil on both sides.
3. Toast the Bread:
   - Place the bread slices on the grill pan or grill, or under the broiler. Toast each side until golden brown and crispy, about 1-2 minutes per side. Watch carefully to prevent burning.
4. Assemble Bruschetta:
   - Arrange the toasted bread slices on a serving platter or tray.
   - Spoon the tomato basil mixture generously over each slice of toasted bread, allowing some of the juices to soak into the bread.
5. Optional Garnish:
   - Drizzle a little balsamic glaze over the top of each bruschetta for extra flavor and presentation, if desired.
6. Serve:
   - Serve the bruschetta immediately as a delightful appetizer or snack. It's best enjoyed fresh when the bread is still warm and crispy.

Bruschetta with Tomato and Basil is a perfect way to showcase the vibrant flavors of summer tomatoes and fresh herbs. It's a versatile dish that can be served at parties, gatherings, or as a light starter to a meal.

Shrimp Cocktail

Ingredients:

For the Shrimp:

- 1 pound large shrimp, peeled and deveined (tails left on or off, as preferred)
- Water, for boiling
- 1 lemon, sliced
- 1 bay leaf
- Salt, to taste

For the Cocktail Sauce:

- 1/2 cup ketchup
- 2 tablespoons prepared horseradish (adjust to taste for spiciness)
- 1 tablespoon fresh lemon juice
- 1 teaspoon Worcestershire sauce
- Hot sauce (such as Tabasco), to taste (optional)
- Salt and pepper, to taste

For Garnish (optional):

- Fresh parsley sprigs
- Lemon wedges

Instructions:

1. Prepare the Shrimp:
    - Fill a large pot with water and add lemon slices, bay leaf, and salt. Bring the water to a boil over high heat.
    - Once boiling, reduce heat to medium-high and add the shrimp. Cook for 2-3 minutes, or until shrimp are pink and opaque.
    - Drain the shrimp and transfer them immediately to a bowl of ice water to cool and stop the cooking process. Once cooled, drain well.
2. Make the Cocktail Sauce:
    - In a small bowl, combine the ketchup, prepared horseradish, fresh lemon juice, Worcestershire sauce, and hot sauce (if using). Mix well to combine.
    - Taste and adjust seasoning with salt, pepper, and additional horseradish or hot sauce, according to your preference for spiciness.
3. Serve:
    - Arrange the chilled shrimp on a serving platter or individual cocktail glasses.
    - Serve the cocktail sauce in a bowl alongside the shrimp.
    - Garnish with fresh parsley sprigs and lemon wedges, if desired.
4. Enjoy:

- Shrimp cocktail is best served chilled. Dip each shrimp into the cocktail sauce before enjoying this classic appetizer.

Shrimp cocktail is elegant yet simple, making it perfect for parties, special occasions, or as a refreshing starter before a meal. Adjust the spiciness of the cocktail sauce to suit your taste preferences for a personalized touch.

Mini Quiches

Ingredients:

For the Quiche Filling:

- 4 large eggs
- 1/2 cup heavy cream
- 1/2 cup milk
- 1/2 cup shredded cheese (such as cheddar, Swiss, or Gruyere)
- 1/2 cup diced cooked ham or bacon (optional)
- 1/4 cup diced onion
- 1/4 cup chopped spinach or other vegetables (optional)
- Salt and pepper, to taste
- Pinch of nutmeg (optional)

For the Quiche Crust:

- 1 sheet of pre-made pie crust or puff pastry, thawed if frozen
- Flour, for dusting

Instructions:

1. Preheat Oven: Preheat your oven to 375°F (190°C). Grease a mini muffin tin or line with paper liners.
2. Prepare the Crust:
   - Roll out the pie crust or puff pastry on a lightly floured surface. Using a round cookie cutter or the rim of a glass, cut out circles slightly larger than the cavities of your mini muffin tin.
   - Press each circle of dough gently into the mini muffin tin cavities, forming little crusts. Trim any excess dough if necessary.
3. Prepare the Filling:
   - In a bowl, whisk together the eggs, heavy cream, and milk until well combined.
   - Stir in the shredded cheese, diced ham or bacon (if using), diced onion, chopped spinach or vegetables (if using), salt, pepper, and nutmeg (if using).
4. Fill the Crusts:
   - Spoon the quiche filling mixture into each mini pie crust, filling them almost to the top.
5. Bake:
   - Bake in the preheated oven for 15-20 minutes, or until the quiches are set and the crusts are golden brown.
6. Cool and Serve:
   - Allow the mini quiches to cool in the muffin tin for a few minutes before carefully removing them. Serve warm or at room temperature.
7. Enjoy:

- Mini quiches can be served as a delicious appetizer or snack. They can also be made ahead and reheated briefly in the oven before serving.

These mini quiches are versatile, and you can customize the fillings with your favorite ingredients such as different cheeses, vegetables, or cooked meats. They are sure to be a hit at any gathering!

Deviled Eggs

Ingredients:

- 6 large eggs
- 2-3 tablespoons mayonnaise
- 1 teaspoon Dijon mustard
- 1/2 teaspoon white vinegar or lemon juice
- Salt and pepper, to taste
- Paprika, for garnish
- Optional: chopped fresh chives or parsley for garnish

Instructions:

1. Boil the Eggs:
    - Place the eggs in a single layer in a saucepan and cover with water.
    - Bring the water to a boil over medium-high heat.
    - Once boiling, cover the saucepan and remove it from the heat. Let the eggs sit in the hot water for 10-12 minutes.
2. Prepare an Ice Bath:
    - While the eggs are cooking, prepare a bowl of ice water.
3. Peel the Eggs:
    - After 10-12 minutes, carefully remove the eggs from the hot water and place them into the ice water bath to cool for a few minutes.
4. Slice and Scoop Out Yolks:
    - Gently peel the eggs and slice them in half lengthwise.
    - Carefully remove the yolks and transfer them to a bowl. Set the egg whites aside on a serving platter.
5. Make the Filling:
    - Mash the egg yolks with a fork until smooth.
    - Add mayonnaise, Dijon mustard, white vinegar or lemon juice, salt, and pepper to the mashed yolks. Mix until well combined and creamy. Adjust the ingredients to taste.
6. Fill the Egg Whites:
    - Spoon or pipe the yolk mixture evenly into the hollows of the egg whites.
7. Garnish:
    - Sprinkle the deviled eggs with paprika for color and optional chopped fresh chives or parsley for garnish.
8. Chill and Serve:
    - Chill the deviled eggs in the refrigerator for at least 30 minutes before serving to allow the flavors to meld.
9. Enjoy:
    - Serve chilled as a delicious appetizer or side dish.

Deviled eggs are versatile, and you can customize them by adding ingredients like chopped pickles, bacon bits, or different herbs and spices. They are perfect for parties, picnics, or any occasion where you want a tasty and satisfying appetizer!

Chicken Satay Skewers

Ingredients:

For the Chicken Satay:

- 1 pound boneless, skinless chicken breasts or thighs, cut into thin strips (about 1-inch wide)
- Wooden skewers, soaked in water for 30 minutes (or metal skewers)

Marinade:

- 1/4 cup coconut milk
- 2 tablespoons soy sauce
- 2 tablespoons fish sauce
- 1 tablespoon brown sugar
- 2 cloves garlic, minced
- 1 teaspoon curry powder
- 1/2 teaspoon turmeric powder
- 1/2 teaspoon ground cumin
- 1/2 teaspoon ground coriander
- 1/4 teaspoon ground ginger
- Pinch of cayenne pepper (optional, for heat)

Peanut Dipping Sauce:

- 1/2 cup creamy peanut butter
- 1/4 cup coconut milk
- 2 tablespoons soy sauce
- 1 tablespoon brown sugar
- 1 tablespoon lime juice
- 1 clove garlic, minced
- 1/2 teaspoon grated fresh ginger
- Pinch of cayenne pepper (optional, for heat)
- Water, as needed to adjust consistency

For Garnish (optional):

- Chopped peanuts
- Fresh cilantro, chopped
- Lime wedges

Instructions:

1. Prepare the Marinade:

        - In a bowl, whisk together coconut milk, soy sauce, fish sauce, brown sugar, minced garlic, curry powder, turmeric powder, cumin, coriander, ginger, and cayenne pepper (if using). Mix until well combined.
 2. Marinate the Chicken:
       - Place the chicken strips in a shallow dish or resealable plastic bag. Pour the marinade over the chicken, ensuring all pieces are well coated. Cover or seal and refrigerate for at least 1 hour, or ideally overnight.
 3. Make the Peanut Dipping Sauce:
       - In a small saucepan over low heat, combine peanut butter, coconut milk, soy sauce, brown sugar, lime juice, minced garlic, grated ginger, and cayenne pepper (if using). Stir continuously until smooth and heated through. If the sauce is too thick, thin it out with a little water until desired consistency is reached. Remove from heat and set aside.
 4. Preheat the Grill or Oven:
       - Preheat your grill or oven broiler to medium-high heat.
 5. Skewer the Chicken:
       - Thread marinated chicken strips onto skewers, leaving a little space between each piece.
 6. Grill or Broil the Chicken:
       - Grill or broil the chicken skewers for about 3-4 minutes per side, or until the chicken is cooked through and nicely charred on the edges. Make sure to turn them halfway through cooking.
 7. Serve:
       - Arrange the grilled chicken satay skewers on a platter.
       - Serve immediately with the peanut dipping sauce on the side.
       - Garnish with chopped peanuts, fresh cilantro, and lime wedges if desired.
 8. Enjoy:
       - Chicken satay skewers are best enjoyed warm as an appetizer or main dish. They pair wonderfully with steamed rice or a fresh salad.

This recipe for chicken satay skewers with peanut dipping sauce brings together savory, sweet, and slightly spicy flavors that are sure to impress your guests!

Spanakopita (Greek Spinach Pie)

Ingredients:

For the Filling:

- 1 pound fresh spinach, washed and chopped (or 10 ounces frozen spinach, thawed and squeezed dry)
- 1/2 pound feta cheese, crumbled
- 1 small onion, finely chopped
- 2 green onions, finely chopped
- 2 cloves garlic, minced
- 1/4 cup fresh dill, chopped (or 1 tablespoon dried dill)
- 1/4 cup fresh parsley, chopped
- 2 tablespoons olive oil
- Salt and pepper, to taste
- Pinch of nutmeg (optional)

For the Phyllo Dough Layers:

- 1/2 pound phyllo dough, thawed if frozen
- 1/2 cup unsalted butter, melted (or olive oil, for brushing)

Instructions:

1. Prepare the Filling:
    - If using fresh spinach, wash and chop it. If using frozen spinach, thaw it completely and squeeze out any excess water using a clean kitchen towel or paper towels.
    - In a large skillet, heat olive oil over medium heat. Add chopped onion and cook until translucent, about 3-4 minutes.
    - Add minced garlic and cook for another 1-2 minutes until fragrant.
    - Add chopped spinach to the skillet and cook until wilted, stirring occasionally. If using fresh spinach, this will take a few minutes. If using frozen spinach, just heat through.
    - Remove from heat and let cool slightly.
    - In a large bowl, combine the spinach mixture with crumbled feta cheese, chopped green onions, chopped dill, chopped parsley, salt, pepper, and a pinch of nutmeg if using. Mix well to combine.
2. Assemble the Spanakopita:
    - Preheat your oven to 350°F (175°C). Lightly grease a 9x13 inch baking dish with butter or olive oil.
    - Lay one sheet of phyllo dough in the prepared baking dish and brush it lightly with melted butter or olive oil. Repeat with 5 more sheets of phyllo dough, brushing each layer with butter or oil.

- Spread the spinach and feta mixture evenly over the layered phyllo dough.
3. Layer More Phyllo Dough:
    - Layer the remaining sheets of phyllo dough over the spinach filling, brushing each sheet with butter or oil as before. Remember to brush the top layer generously to ensure a crispy crust.
4. Bake the Spanakopita:
    - Using a sharp knife, score the top layer of phyllo dough into squares or triangles. This will make it easier to cut after baking.
    - Bake in the preheated oven for 45-55 minutes, or until the top is golden brown and crispy.
5. Cool and Serve:
    - Remove from the oven and let cool for a few minutes before cutting into squares or triangles along the scored lines.
    - Spanakopita can be served warm or at room temperature. Enjoy this delicious Greek spinach pie as a main dish or appetizer!

Spanakopita is a versatile dish that can be enjoyed on its own or paired with a fresh salad for a complete meal. It's perfect for gatherings and celebrations, showcasing the wonderful flavors of spinach, herbs, and feta cheese wrapped in flaky phyllo dough.

Cheese Stuffed Jalapeños

Ingredients:

- 12 fresh jalapeño peppers
- 8 ounces cream cheese, softened
- 1 cup shredded cheddar cheese (or your favorite melting cheese)
- 1/2 teaspoon garlic powder
- 1/2 teaspoon onion powder
- Salt and pepper, to taste
- 1/2 cup breadcrumbs (plain or seasoned)
- Optional: 6 slices of bacon, cooked and crumbled

Instructions:

1. Prepare the Jalapeños:
    - Preheat your oven to 375°F (190°C). Line a baking sheet with parchment paper.
    - Cut each jalapeño pepper in half lengthwise and remove the seeds and membranes. Use a small spoon or knife to scrape out the seeds and white pith. Wear gloves or wash your hands thoroughly afterward, as jalapeños can be spicy and can irritate skin.
2. Make the Filling:
    - In a mixing bowl, combine softened cream cheese, shredded cheddar cheese, garlic powder, onion powder, salt, and pepper. Optionally, mix in crumbled bacon for extra flavor.
3. Stuff the Jalapeños:
    - Spoon the cheese mixture evenly into each jalapeño half, filling them to the top.
4. Coat with Breadcrumbs:
    - Place breadcrumbs in a shallow bowl. Press the filled jalapeños, cheese side down, into the breadcrumbs to coat the top generously.
5. Bake the Jalapeño Poppers:
    - Arrange the stuffed jalapeños on the prepared baking sheet, cheese side up.
    - Bake in the preheated oven for 20-25 minutes, or until the jalapeños are tender and the cheese is melted and bubbly, and the breadcrumbs are golden brown.
6. Serve:
    - Remove from the oven and let cool for a few minutes before serving. Arrange on a platter and serve warm.
7. Enjoy:
    - Cheese stuffed jalapeños are best enjoyed warm and can be served as an appetizer or snack. They are perfect for parties, game nights, or any occasion where you want to spice things up a bit!

These cheese stuffed jalapeños are customizable—you can adjust the level of spiciness by removing all or some of the jalapeño seeds and membranes. They are sure to be a hit with anyone who enjoys a bit of heat and cheesy goodness!

Crab Cakes

Ingredients:

- 1 pound lump crab meat, picked over for shells
- 1/3 cup mayonnaise
- 1 large egg, beaten
- 1 tablespoon Dijon mustard
- 1 tablespoon Worcestershire sauce
- 1 teaspoon Old Bay seasoning (or seafood seasoning of your choice)
- 1/4 teaspoon salt
- 1/4 teaspoon black pepper
- 1/2 cup panko breadcrumbs (plus more for coating)
- 2 tablespoons chopped fresh parsley
- 1/4 cup finely chopped red bell pepper (optional, for added flavor and color)
- 2 tablespoons unsalted butter
- 2 tablespoons olive oil

Instructions:

1. Prepare the Crab Cakes Mixture:
    - In a large mixing bowl, combine the mayonnaise, beaten egg, Dijon mustard, Worcestershire sauce, Old Bay seasoning, salt, and black pepper. Mix well.
    - Gently fold in the lump crab meat, panko breadcrumbs, chopped parsley, and finely chopped red bell pepper (if using). Be careful not to break up the crab meat too much.
2. Form the Crab Cakes:
    - Divide the crab mixture into 8 equal portions. Shape each portion into a patty about 1 inch thick. Place the formed crab cakes on a plate or baking sheet lined with parchment paper.
3. Coat the Crab Cakes:
    - Spread some additional panko breadcrumbs on a plate. Carefully coat each crab cake patty with breadcrumbs, pressing lightly to adhere. This helps create a crispy crust when cooking.
4. Cook the Crab Cakes:
    - In a large skillet, heat 1 tablespoon of butter and 1 tablespoon of olive oil over medium heat.
    - Add the crab cakes to the skillet (in batches if necessary to avoid overcrowding). Cook for about 4-5 minutes on each side, or until golden brown and heated through. Add more butter and oil to the skillet as needed for subsequent batches.
    - Transfer the cooked crab cakes to a paper towel-lined plate to drain any excess oil.
5. Serve:

- Serve the crab cakes warm with your favorite dipping sauce, such as tartar sauce, remoulade, or a squeeze of lemon wedges.
6. Enjoy:
    - Crab cakes are delicious as an appetizer, main course, or as part of a seafood platter. Enjoy the delicate flavors of crab with a crispy exterior—perfect for any occasion!

These crab cakes are sure to impress with their rich seafood flavor and crispy texture. Adjust the seasoning and ingredients to suit your taste preferences, and serve them as a delightful treat for seafood lovers.

Meatballs with BBQ Sauce

Ingredients:

For the Meatballs:

- 1 pound ground beef (or a mix of beef and pork)
- 1/2 cup breadcrumbs
- 1/4 cup grated Parmesan cheese
- 1/4 cup milk
- 1 small onion, finely chopped
- 2 cloves garlic, minced
- 1 large egg
- 1 tablespoon Worcestershire sauce
- 1 teaspoon dried oregano
- 1 teaspoon dried basil
- Salt and pepper, to taste
- Olive oil, for cooking

For the BBQ Sauce:

- 1 cup BBQ sauce (use your favorite brand or homemade)
- 1/4 cup ketchup
- 2 tablespoons brown sugar
- 1 tablespoon apple cider vinegar
- 1 teaspoon smoked paprika (optional, for extra smoky flavor)
- Salt and pepper, to taste

For Garnish:

- Fresh parsley or chives, chopped (optional)

Instructions:

1. Preheat the Oven:
    - Preheat your oven to 400°F (200°C). Line a baking sheet with parchment paper or foil for easy cleanup.
2. Make the Meatballs:
    - In a large bowl, combine ground beef, breadcrumbs, grated Parmesan cheese, milk, chopped onion, minced garlic, egg, Worcestershire sauce, dried oregano, dried basil, salt, and pepper. Mix until well combined.
    - Shape the mixture into meatballs, about 1 to 1.5 inches in diameter. You should get approximately 20-24 meatballs.
3. Cook the Meatballs:

- Heat a drizzle of olive oil in a large skillet over medium-high heat. Brown the meatballs on all sides, working in batches if necessary to avoid overcrowding the pan. This should take about 6-8 minutes per batch.
4. Make the BBQ Sauce:
    - While the meatballs are browning, prepare the BBQ sauce. In a small saucepan, combine BBQ sauce, ketchup, brown sugar, apple cider vinegar, smoked paprika (if using), salt, and pepper. Stir well and bring to a simmer over medium heat. Cook for 5 minutes, stirring occasionally, until the sauce has thickened slightly.
5. Combine and Bake:
    - Transfer the browned meatballs to the prepared baking sheet. Brush each meatball generously with the prepared BBQ sauce, reserving some sauce for serving.
    - Bake in the preheated oven for 15-20 minutes, or until the meatballs are cooked through and the sauce is caramelized.
6. Serve:
    - Remove from the oven and let the meatballs cool slightly. Garnish with chopped parsley or chives if desired.
    - Serve the BBQ meatballs warm with extra BBQ sauce on the side for dipping or drizzling.
7. Enjoy:
    - These BBQ meatballs are perfect for serving as an appetizer with toothpicks or as a main dish with sides like mashed potatoes or coleslaw. They're sure to be a hit at any gathering or family meal!

These meatballs with BBQ sauce are versatile and can be made ahead of time and reheated before serving. Adjust the sweetness or spiciness of the BBQ sauce to your preference for a personalized touch.

Cucumber Bites with Herbed Cream Cheese

Ingredients:

- 1 English cucumber (or 2-3 smaller cucumbers)
- 8 ounces cream cheese, softened
- 2 tablespoons fresh dill, chopped
- 2 tablespoons fresh chives, chopped
- 1 tablespoon fresh parsley, chopped
- 1 clove garlic, minced
- Salt and pepper, to taste
- Optional: Lemon zest or lemon juice for extra freshness
- Optional: Cherry tomatoes or olives for garnish

Instructions:

1. Prepare the Cucumbers:
    - Wash the cucumber(s) thoroughly. If using English cucumber, leave the skin on for a nice contrast in color and texture. If using smaller cucumbers, you may peel them if desired.
    - Slice the cucumber(s) into 1/4 to 1/2 inch thick rounds. Place the slices on a paper towel-lined tray to absorb excess moisture. Pat them dry with another paper towel on top.
2. Make the Herbed Cream Cheese:
    - In a mixing bowl, combine softened cream cheese, chopped fresh dill, chives, parsley, minced garlic, salt, and pepper. Mix well until the herbs are evenly distributed throughout the cream cheese.
    - Optionally, add a touch of lemon zest or a squeeze of lemon juice for extra freshness.
3. Assemble the Cucumber Bites:
    - Take each cucumber round and spread a small amount (about 1 teaspoon) of herbed cream cheese on top, covering the surface.
    - Optionally, you can use a piping bag fitted with a star tip to pipe the herbed cream cheese onto the cucumber slices for a decorative touch.
4. Garnish (Optional):
    - Garnish each cucumber bite with a small piece of cherry tomato, olive, or additional fresh herbs for added flavor and presentation.
5. Serve:
    - Arrange the cucumber bites on a serving platter and serve immediately, or cover and refrigerate until ready to serve. They are best served chilled.
6. Enjoy:
    - These cucumber bites with herbed cream cheese are light, flavorful, and perfect for any gathering. They're a great option for those looking for a refreshing and low-carb appetizer.

These cucumber bites can be customized with your favorite herbs or additional toppings like smoked salmon or shrimp for extra elegance. They're sure to impress your guests with their bright flavors and elegant presentation!

Antipasto Skewers

Ingredients:

- Cherry tomatoes
- Mozzarella balls (bocconcini)
- Salami slices, folded or rolled
- Black or green olives, pitted
- Artichoke hearts, drained and halved
- Basil leaves
- Balsamic glaze, for drizzling (optional)
- Wooden skewers or toothpicks

Instructions:

1. Prepare Ingredients:
   - If using wooden skewers, soak them in water for 30 minutes to prevent them from burning during cooking.
2. Assemble Skewers:
   - Start assembling the skewers by threading the ingredients onto the skewers in any order you prefer. A suggested order could be: cherry tomato, folded salami slice, mozzarella ball, olive, artichoke heart half, and basil leaf. Repeat until the skewer is full, leaving a little space at each end for easy handling.
3. Arrange and Serve:
   - Place the assembled antipasto skewers on a serving platter.
   - Optional: Drizzle the skewers with balsamic glaze for an extra burst of flavor.
4. Serve:
   - Serve the antipasto skewers immediately as an appetizer or part of a larger antipasto platter.
   - Enjoy the combination of flavors and textures!

These antipasto skewers are versatile, and you can customize them with your favorite antipasto ingredients such as marinated artichoke hearts, roasted red peppers, or even prosciutto. They're perfect for parties, gatherings, or as a delicious snack any time!

Smoked Salmon Canapés

Ingredients:

- Slices of baguette or cocktail bread, toasted or untoasted (depending on preference)
- Smoked salmon slices, thinly sliced
- Cream cheese or goat cheese, softened
- Fresh dill, chopped
- Capers, drained
- Lemon zest or lemon juice
- Black pepper, freshly ground

Instructions:

1. Prepare the Bread:
    - Slice the baguette into thin rounds or use pre-sliced cocktail bread. Toast the bread slices lightly if desired, or leave them untoasted for a softer texture.
2. Prepare the Cream Cheese Spread:
    - In a small bowl, mix the softened cream cheese or goat cheese with chopped fresh dill. Optionally, add a dash of lemon zest or a squeeze of lemon juice for added brightness.
3. Assemble the Canapés:
    - Spread a thin layer of the cream cheese mixture onto each slice of bread.
4. Add the Smoked Salmon:
    - Top each bread slice with a slice of smoked salmon, folding or arranging it attractively on top of the cream cheese.
5. Garnish:
    - Sprinkle a few capers over the smoked salmon.
6. Season:
    - Finish each canapé with a sprinkle of freshly ground black pepper.
7. Serve:
    - Arrange the smoked salmon canapés on a serving platter.
8. Enjoy:
    - Serve immediately and enjoy these elegant and flavorful smoked salmon canapés as a sophisticated appetizer.

These smoked salmon canapés are not only delicious but also visually appealing, making them a great addition to any party or gathering. You can customize them by adding additional garnishes like thinly sliced cucumber, red onion, or a drizzle of balsamic glaze for extra flavor. They're sure to impress your guests with their combination of creamy cheese, delicate smoked salmon, and fresh herbs!

Buffalo Cauliflower Bites

Ingredients:

- 1 head of cauliflower, cut into bite-sized florets
- 1 cup all-purpose flour (or substitute with almond flour for a gluten-free option)
- 1 cup milk (or plant-based milk for a vegan option)
- 1 teaspoon garlic powder
- 1 teaspoon paprika
- 1/2 teaspoon salt
- 1/4 teaspoon black pepper
- 1 cup buffalo sauce (such as Frank's RedHot or your favorite brand)
- 2 tablespoons unsalted butter or margarine (use vegan butter for a vegan option)
- Optional: Ranch or blue cheese dressing, for dipping
- Optional: Chopped fresh parsley or chives, for garnish

Instructions:

1. Preheat the Oven:
    - Preheat your oven to 450°F (230°C). Line a baking sheet with parchment paper or lightly grease it.
2. Prepare the Cauliflower:
    - Cut the cauliflower into bite-sized florets, discarding the tough stem.
3. Prepare the Batter:
    - In a mixing bowl, whisk together the flour, milk, garlic powder, paprika, salt, and black pepper until smooth and well combined.
4. Coat the Cauliflower:
    - Dip each cauliflower floret into the batter, ensuring it's well coated. Shake off any excess batter and place the coated florets on the prepared baking sheet in a single layer, leaving space between each piece.
5. Bake the Cauliflower:
    - Bake in the preheated oven for 20-25 minutes, or until the cauliflower is golden brown and crispy. You may need to flip the florets halfway through baking for even browning.
6. Prepare the Buffalo Sauce:
    - While the cauliflower is baking, melt the butter in a small saucepan over low heat. Once melted, stir in the buffalo sauce until well combined. Simmer for a few minutes to let the flavors meld together.
7. Coat the Cauliflower with Buffalo Sauce:
    - Remove the cauliflower from the oven and carefully transfer the hot florets to a large mixing bowl.
    - Pour the buffalo sauce mixture over the cauliflower and gently toss until all florets are evenly coated.
8. Serve:

        - Transfer the buffalo cauliflower bites to a serving platter. Optionally, garnish with chopped fresh parsley or chives.
9. Enjoy:
        - Serve immediately with ranch or blue cheese dressing on the side for dipping. These buffalo cauliflower bites are best enjoyed warm and are sure to be a hit at parties or as a delicious snack!

These buffalo cauliflower bites are crispy, spicy, and addictive, making them a popular choice for both vegetarians and anyone who loves a tasty buffalo wing alternative. Adjust the spice level by varying the amount of buffalo sauce used according to your preference.

Baked Brie with Jam

Ingredients:

- 1 round of Brie cheese (about 8-10 ounces)
- 1/4 cup fruit preserves or jam (such as fig, apricot, raspberry, or cranberry)
- 1/4 cup chopped nuts (optional, such as pecans or almonds)
- Fresh thyme or rosemary sprigs, for garnish
- Crackers or bread slices, for serving

Instructions:

1. Preheat the Oven:
    - Preheat your oven to 350°F (175°C).
2. Prepare the Brie:
    - Place the Brie round on a baking sheet lined with parchment paper or in a small baking dish. Leave the rind on for baking.
3. Add the Jam:
    - Spread the fruit preserves or jam evenly over the top of the Brie round. You can use a spoon to gently spread it out, covering the top surface.
4. Optional: Add Nuts:
    - Sprinkle chopped nuts over the jam-covered Brie for added texture and flavor.
5. Bake the Brie:
    - Bake in the preheated oven for 12-15 minutes, or until the Brie is softened and gooey inside. The cheese should be warm and slightly melted but not completely runny.
6. Garnish and Serve:
    - Remove from the oven and let the baked Brie rest for a few minutes. Garnish with fresh thyme or rosemary sprigs for added aroma and presentation.
7. Serve:
    - Serve the baked Brie immediately while warm, accompanied by crackers or bread slices for spreading. Guests can scoop out the melted cheese with crackers or bread.
8. Enjoy:
    - Enjoy the creamy, gooey goodness of baked Brie with the sweet contrast of fruit preserves or jam. It's a perfect appetizer for parties, holidays, or any gathering.

Baked Brie with jam is a versatile dish that can be customized with your favorite flavors. Experiment with different types of fruit preserves or jams to find your favorite combination. It's sure to be a hit and will disappear quickly from the appetizer table!

Mini Crab Salad Cups

Ingredients:

- 1 pound lump crab meat, picked over for shells
- 1/2 cup mayonnaise
- 1/4 cup Greek yogurt (or sour cream)
- 1 tablespoon Dijon mustard
- 1 tablespoon lemon juice
- 1/4 cup finely chopped celery
- 2 tablespoons finely chopped red onion
- 1 tablespoon chopped fresh parsley
- Salt and pepper, to taste
- Mini phyllo cups (available pre-made in the frozen section of most grocery stores)
- Optional: Fresh dill or chives for garnish

Instructions:

1. Prepare the Crab Salad:
   - In a mixing bowl, combine mayonnaise, Greek yogurt (or sour cream), Dijon mustard, and lemon juice. Mix well until smooth.
2. Add Ingredients to Crab Salad:
   - Gently fold in the lump crab meat, chopped celery, chopped red onion, and chopped parsley until well combined. Season with salt and pepper to taste.
3. Prepare the Phyllo Cups:
   - Arrange the mini phyllo cups on a serving platter or baking sheet.
4. Fill the Phyllo Cups:
   - Spoon a small amount of the crab salad mixture into each mini phyllo cup, filling them almost to the top.
5. Garnish (Optional):
   - Garnish each crab salad cup with a small sprig of fresh dill or chopped chives for added flavor and presentation.
6. Serve:
   - Arrange the mini crab salad cups on a serving platter and serve immediately. They are best enjoyed fresh to maintain the crispy texture of the phyllo cups.
7. Enjoy:
   - These mini crab salad cups are perfect for parties, brunches, or any special occasion. They offer a delicious blend of flavors and textures that are sure to impress your guests!

These appetizers can be prepared ahead of time, but it's best to fill the phyllo cups shortly before serving to keep them crispy. Enjoy the delightful combination of crab salad in a bite-sized, elegant presentation!

Spring Rolls with Dipping Sauce

Ingredients:

For the Spring Rolls:

- 8-10 spring roll wrappers (rice paper)
- 1 cup cooked shrimp, peeled and deveined, sliced in half lengthwise
- 1 cup vermicelli noodles, cooked according to package instructions
- 1 cup shredded lettuce or cabbage
- 1 cup matchstick carrots
- 1 cup cucumber, thinly sliced into strips
- Fresh herbs (such as mint, cilantro, and/or Thai basil)
- Optional: Cooked chicken, tofu strips, or additional vegetables of your choice

For the Dipping Sauce:

- 1/4 cup soy sauce
- 2 tablespoons rice vinegar
- 1 tablespoon honey or brown sugar
- 1 clove garlic, minced
- 1 teaspoon grated ginger
- 1 teaspoon sesame oil
- Optional: Sriracha or chili garlic sauce, for spice

Instructions:

1. Prepare the Dipping Sauce:
   - In a small bowl, whisk together soy sauce, rice vinegar, honey or brown sugar, minced garlic, grated ginger, sesame oil, and optional Sriracha or chili garlic sauce. Adjust seasoning to taste. Set aside.
2. Prepare the Spring Roll Fillings:
   - Prepare all the fillings: Slice the cooked shrimp in half lengthwise, cook and cool vermicelli noodles, shred lettuce or cabbage, prepare matchstick carrots, and thinly slice cucumber into strips.
   - Arrange the fillings and fresh herbs on a large plate or workspace for easy assembly.
3. Assemble the Spring Rolls:
   - Fill a shallow dish with warm water. Working with one spring roll wrapper at a time, dip the wrapper into the water for a few seconds until it softens and becomes pliable (do not soak too long).
   - Place the softened wrapper on a clean work surface. Place a small amount of each filling ingredient and fresh herbs in the center of the wrapper, leaving space on the sides.

- Fold the sides of the wrapper over the filling, then fold the bottom edge over the filling tightly. Roll up from the bottom to enclose the filling completely, similar to rolling a burrito. Repeat with remaining wrappers and filling ingredients.
4. Serve the Spring Rolls:
    - Arrange the assembled spring rolls on a serving platter. You can serve them whole or slice them in half diagonally for a decorative presentation.
5. Serve with Dipping Sauce:
    - Serve the spring rolls with the prepared dipping sauce on the side in small bowls or ramekins.
6. Enjoy:
    - Enjoy these fresh and delicious homemade spring rolls with your favorite dipping sauce! They are perfect as an appetizer, light lunch, or party snack.

Spring rolls are versatile, and you can customize the fillings according to your preferences or dietary restrictions. They are also great for making ahead of time and storing in the refrigerator until ready to serve. The dipping sauce adds a savory and tangy flavor that complements the freshness of the spring rolls perfectly.

Gougeres (Cheese Puffs)

Ingredients:

- 1/2 cup water
- 1/2 cup whole milk
- 8 tablespoons unsalted butter (1 stick), cut into pieces
- 1/2 teaspoon salt
- 1 cup all-purpose flour
- 4 large eggs, at room temperature
- 1 1/2 cups grated Gruyère cheese (or other Swiss cheese), divided
- Freshly ground black pepper, to taste
- Optional: Pinch of cayenne pepper or nutmeg for a subtle spice (optional)

Instructions:

1. Preheat the Oven:
    - Preheat your oven to 400°F (200°C). Line a baking sheet with parchment paper or lightly grease it.
2. Prepare the Dough:
    - In a medium saucepan, combine water, milk, butter, and salt. Bring to a simmer over medium heat, stirring occasionally, until the butter melts completely.
3. Add the Flour:
    - Reduce the heat to low and add the flour all at once. Stir vigorously with a wooden spoon until the mixture forms a smooth dough and pulls away from the sides of the pan, about 1-2 minutes. Remove from heat.
4. Incorporate Eggs:
    - Let the dough cool for a few minutes. Add the eggs one at a time, beating well after each addition, until the dough is smooth and glossy. It may look like it's separating at first, but continue beating until it comes together.
5. Add Cheese and Seasoning:
    - Stir in 1 cup of grated Gruyère cheese and season with black pepper (and cayenne or nutmeg if using), mixing until evenly incorporated.
6. Form and Bake Gougères:
    - Drop spoonfuls of dough onto the prepared baking sheet, spacing them about 2 inches apart. Alternatively, you can use a piping bag fitted with a plain tip to pipe the dough into small mounds.
7. Top with Cheese:
    - Sprinkle the remaining 1/2 cup of grated Gruyère cheese evenly over the tops of the gougères.
8. Bake:
    - Bake in the preheated oven for 20-25 minutes, or until the gougères are puffed and golden brown.
9. Serve:

- Remove from the oven and let cool slightly on the baking sheet. Serve warm or at room temperature.
10. Enjoy:
    - Gougères are best enjoyed fresh and warm, with their cheesy goodness. They can be served as appetizers or snacks alongside a glass of wine or champagne.

These gougères are versatile and can be filled with various savory ingredients like herbs, bacon bits, or even finely chopped vegetables for added flavor. They're sure to impress your guests with their light and airy texture and cheesy aroma!

Chicken Wings (Various Flavors)

BBQ Chicken Wings:

Ingredients:

- 2 pounds chicken wings, split at the joint and tips removed
- Salt and pepper, to taste
- 1 cup BBQ sauce (your favorite brand or homemade)
- 2 tablespoons unsalted butter, melted
- 1 tablespoon honey
- Optional: Chopped fresh cilantro or parsley for garnish

Instructions:

1. Preheat the Oven:
   - Preheat your oven to 400°F (200°C). Line a baking sheet with parchment paper.
2. Prepare the Chicken Wings:
   - Pat dry the chicken wings with paper towels. Season with salt and pepper to taste.
3. Bake the Wings:
   - Arrange the chicken wings in a single layer on the prepared baking sheet. Bake for 35-40 minutes, turning once halfway through, or until golden brown and crispy.
4. Make the BBQ Sauce:
   - In a small bowl, mix together BBQ sauce, melted butter, and honey until well combined.
5. Coat the Wings:
   - Remove the wings from the oven and brush them generously with the BBQ sauce mixture. Return to the oven and bake for an additional 5-10 minutes, or until the sauce is sticky and caramelized.
6. Garnish and Serve:
   - Remove from the oven and garnish with chopped fresh cilantro or parsley if desired. Serve warm.

Buffalo Chicken Wings:

Ingredients:

- 2 pounds chicken wings, split at the joint and tips removed
- Salt and pepper, to taste
- 1/2 cup hot sauce (such as Frank's RedHot)
- 1/4 cup unsalted butter, melted
- 1 tablespoon white vinegar
- Optional: Blue cheese or ranch dressing, celery sticks for serving

Instructions:

1. Preheat the Oven:
    - Preheat your oven to 400°F (200°C). Line a baking sheet with parchment paper.
2. Prepare the Chicken Wings:
    - Pat dry the chicken wings with paper towels. Season with salt and pepper to taste.
3. Bake the Wings:
    - Arrange the chicken wings in a single layer on the prepared baking sheet. Bake for 35-40 minutes, turning once halfway through, or until golden brown and crispy.
4. Make the Buffalo Sauce:
    - In a mixing bowl, whisk together hot sauce, melted butter, and white vinegar until well combined.
5. Toss the Wings:
    - Transfer the baked wings to a large bowl. Pour the buffalo sauce over the wings and toss until evenly coated.
6. Serve:
    - Arrange the buffalo wings on a serving platter. Serve with blue cheese or ranch dressing for dipping and celery sticks on the side.

Honey Garlic Chicken Wings:

Ingredients:

- 2 pounds chicken wings, split at the joint and tips removed
- Salt and pepper, to taste
- 1/3 cup honey
- 1/4 cup soy sauce
- 3 cloves garlic, minced
- 1 tablespoon rice vinegar
- Optional: Sesame seeds, chopped green onions for garnish

Instructions:

1. Preheat the Oven:
    - Preheat your oven to 400°F (200°C). Line a baking sheet with parchment paper.
2. Prepare the Chicken Wings:
    - Pat dry the chicken wings with paper towels. Season with salt and pepper to taste.
3. Bake the Wings:
    - Arrange the chicken wings in a single layer on the prepared baking sheet. Bake for 35-40 minutes, turning once halfway through, or until golden brown and crispy.
4. Make the Honey Garlic Sauce:

- In a small saucepan, combine honey, soy sauce, minced garlic, and rice vinegar. Bring to a simmer over medium heat, stirring occasionally, for about 5 minutes or until slightly thickened.
5. Coat the Wings:
    - Transfer the baked wings to a large bowl. Pour the honey garlic sauce over the wings and toss until evenly coated.
6. Garnish and Serve:
    - Arrange the honey garlic wings on a serving platter. Sprinkle with sesame seeds and chopped green onions if desired. Serve warm.

These chicken wing recipes are perfect for game day, parties, or any occasion where you want to enjoy delicious finger food with friends and family. Adjust the spice level and seasonings according to your taste preferences for a personalized touch!

Avocado Shrimp Cups

Ingredients:

- 12 large shrimp, peeled and deveined
- 1 avocado, ripe yet firm
- 1 tablespoon lime juice (about 1 lime)
- Salt and pepper, to taste
- 1/4 cup cherry tomatoes, diced
- 2 tablespoons red onion, finely chopped
- 1 tablespoon cilantro, chopped
- 1 tablespoon olive oil
- Optional: Dash of hot sauce or chili flakes for a kick
- Optional: Tortilla chips or lettuce leaves for serving

Instructions:

1. Prepare the Shrimp:
    - Bring a pot of water to a boil. Add the shrimp and cook for 2-3 minutes until pink and opaque. Drain and rinse under cold water to stop the cooking process. Pat dry with paper towels.
2. Prepare the Avocado:
    - Cut the avocado in half lengthwise and remove the pit. Scoop out the flesh into a medium bowl. Mash the avocado with a fork until smooth with some chunks remaining.
3. Season the Avocado:
    - Add lime juice, salt, and pepper to taste to the mashed avocado. Mix well to combine.
4. Prepare the Shrimp Mixture:
    - Chop the cooked shrimp into bite-sized pieces and add them to a separate bowl. Add diced cherry tomatoes, finely chopped red onion, chopped cilantro, and olive oil. Season with salt and pepper to taste. Optionally, add a dash of hot sauce or chili flakes for extra spice.
5. Combine Avocado and Shrimp:
    - Gently fold the shrimp mixture into the mashed avocado until evenly combined.
6. Assemble the Cups:
    - Spoon the avocado shrimp mixture into small serving cups or hollowed-out avocado halves for a creative presentation.
7. Serve:
    - Serve the avocado shrimp cups immediately, garnished with additional cilantro if desired. Optionally, serve with tortilla chips or lettuce leaves for scooping.
8. Enjoy:

- These avocado shrimp cups are best enjoyed fresh and are perfect as a light appetizer or snack. They are also great for entertaining and can be prepared ahead of time and assembled just before serving.

These avocado shrimp cups are not only delicious but also packed with healthy fats and protein, making them a nutritious choice for any occasion. Customize them by adding your favorite herbs or adjusting the seasoning to suit your taste preferences.

Stuffed Mini Peppers

Ingredients:

- 12 mini bell peppers, halved and seeds removed
- 4 oz cream cheese, softened
- 1/2 cup shredded cheddar cheese (or cheese of your choice)
- 1/4 cup finely chopped red onion
- 1/4 cup chopped fresh parsley or cilantro
- 1/2 teaspoon garlic powder
- Salt and pepper, to taste
- Optional: Crumbled bacon, diced jalapeño, or other fillings of your choice

Instructions:

1. Preheat the Oven:
    - Preheat your oven to 375°F (190°C). Line a baking sheet with parchment paper or lightly grease it.
2. Prepare the Peppers:
    - Slice the mini bell peppers in half lengthwise and remove the seeds and membranes.
3. Make the Filling:
    - In a mixing bowl, combine softened cream cheese, shredded cheddar cheese, finely chopped red onion, chopped fresh parsley or cilantro, garlic powder, salt, and pepper. Mix well until smooth and evenly combined. Adjust seasoning to taste.
4. Fill the Peppers:
    - Spoon the cheese mixture evenly into each pepper half, pressing gently to fill any cavities. Optionally, you can add crumbled bacon, diced jalapeño, or other fillings on top of the cheese mixture.
5. Bake the Stuffed Peppers:
    - Place the stuffed mini peppers on the prepared baking sheet. Bake in the preheated oven for 15-20 minutes, or until the peppers are tender and the filling is heated through and lightly golden on top.
6. Serve:
    - Remove from the oven and let cool slightly. Arrange the stuffed mini peppers on a serving platter and serve warm.
7. Enjoy:
    - These stuffed mini peppers are perfect as a party appetizer or snack. They are colorful, flavorful, and can be easily customized with your favorite ingredients. Serve them fresh out of the oven for the best taste and texture!

Feel free to experiment with different fillings and cheeses to create variations of stuffed mini peppers that suit your taste preferences. They are sure to be a hit at any gathering or as a tasty snack any time!

Prosciutto-Wrapped Melon

Ingredients:

- 1 ripe cantaloupe or honeydew melon
- 6-8 slices of prosciutto
- Fresh basil leaves (optional, for garnish)
- Balsamic glaze (optional, for drizzling)

Instructions:

1. Prepare the Melon:
    - Cut the cantaloupe or honeydew melon in half and remove the seeds. Slice the melon into wedges or bite-sized cubes, depending on your preference.
2. Wrap with Prosciutto:
    - Cut each slice of prosciutto in half lengthwise to make thinner strips. Wrap each strip around a melon wedge or cube. You can secure with a toothpick if needed, but it's not necessary.
3. Arrange on a Platter:
    - Arrange the prosciutto-wrapped melon pieces on a serving platter. If using basil leaves, tuck them between the melon and prosciutto for added flavor and decoration.
4. Optional Garnish:
    - Drizzle the prosciutto-wrapped melon with balsamic glaze for an extra touch of sweetness and acidity.
5. Serve:
    - Serve the prosciutto-wrapped melon immediately as an appetizer or part of a charcuterie board. Enjoy the contrast of flavors between the sweet melon and salty prosciutto!

Prosciutto-wrapped melon is a quick and easy appetizer that is perfect for parties, gatherings, or even as a light snack. It pairs well with a variety of wines and is sure to impress your guests with its simplicity and delicious taste. Adjust the sweetness of the melon and the saltiness of the prosciutto to your liking for a personalized experience.

Tomato Basil Bruschetta

Ingredients:

- 4-5 ripe tomatoes, diced
- 1/4 cup fresh basil leaves, thinly sliced (chiffonade)
- 2 cloves garlic, minced
- 2 tablespoons extra virgin olive oil
- 1 tablespoon balsamic vinegar
- Salt and freshly ground black pepper, to taste
- 1 French baguette, sliced into 1/2 inch thick rounds
- Olive oil, for brushing the bread

Instructions:

1. Prepare the Tomatoes and Basil:
    - In a mixing bowl, combine diced tomatoes, thinly sliced basil leaves, minced garlic, extra virgin olive oil, and balsamic vinegar. Season with salt and pepper to taste. Mix well and set aside to marinate for about 15-20 minutes to allow the flavors to meld together.
2. Prepare the Baguette:
    - Preheat the oven to 375°F (190°C). Arrange the baguette slices on a baking sheet in a single layer. Brush each slice lightly with olive oil on both sides.
3. Toast the Bread:
    - Bake the bread slices in the preheated oven for 8-10 minutes, or until golden brown and crispy. You can also toast them on a grill or in a toaster oven if preferred.
4. Assemble the Bruschetta:
    - Arrange the toasted baguette slices on a serving platter or tray. Spoon the tomato basil mixture generously onto each slice, allowing some of the juices to soak into the bread.
5. Optional Garnish:
    - Garnish the tomato basil bruschetta with additional basil leaves and a drizzle of balsamic glaze if desired.
6. Serve:
    - Serve the tomato basil bruschetta immediately as an appetizer or part of a larger spread. Enjoy the vibrant flavors and textures of this classic Italian dish!

Tomato basil bruschetta is best enjoyed fresh, so assemble it shortly before serving to maintain the crispiness of the bread and the freshness of the tomatoes and basil. It's a versatile dish that can be served at parties, gatherings, or as a delicious starter to a meal. Adjust the seasoning and ingredients according to your taste preferences for a personalized touch!

Asian Meatball Lettuce Wraps

Ingredients:

For the Meatballs:

- 1 pound ground chicken or pork
- 1/4 cup breadcrumbs
- 1 egg
- 2 cloves garlic, minced
- 1 tablespoon ginger, minced
- 2 green onions, finely chopped
- 1 tablespoon soy sauce
- 1 tablespoon hoisin sauce
- 1 teaspoon sesame oil
- Salt and pepper, to taste
- Cooking oil (for frying or baking)

For the Sauce:

- 1/4 cup hoisin sauce
- 2 tablespoons soy sauce
- 1 tablespoon rice vinegar
- 1 tablespoon honey or brown sugar
- 1 teaspoon sesame oil
- Optional: Sriracha or chili garlic sauce, to taste

For Serving:

- Butter lettuce leaves (or any lettuce with large, sturdy leaves)
- Thinly sliced cucumber
- Shredded carrots
- Fresh cilantro leaves
- Toasted sesame seeds (optional)

Instructions:

1. Prepare the Meatballs:
    - In a mixing bowl, combine ground chicken or pork, breadcrumbs, egg, minced garlic, minced ginger, chopped green onions, soy sauce, hoisin sauce, sesame oil, salt, and pepper. Mix until well combined.
2. Form the Meatballs:
    - Shape the mixture into small meatballs, about 1 inch in diameter. You should get around 20-24 meatballs, depending on size.
3. Cook the Meatballs:

- Option 1 (Pan-Fry): Heat a bit of cooking oil in a large skillet over medium heat. Add the meatballs in batches and cook for about 8-10 minutes, turning occasionally, until browned and cooked through.
- Option 2 (Bake): Preheat the oven to 400°F (200°C). Place the meatballs on a baking sheet lined with parchment paper. Bake for 15-20 minutes, or until cooked through and browned.

4. Make the Sauce:
   - In a small bowl, whisk together hoisin sauce, soy sauce, rice vinegar, honey or brown sugar, sesame oil, and optional Sriracha or chili garlic sauce.
5. Assemble the Lettuce Wraps:
   - Arrange the lettuce leaves on a serving platter. Place a few meatballs in each lettuce leaf.
6. Add Toppings:
   - Top the meatballs with thinly sliced cucumber, shredded carrots, fresh cilantro leaves, and optional toasted sesame seeds.
7. Serve:
   - Drizzle the meatballs and toppings with the prepared sauce or serve the sauce on the side for dipping. Enjoy the Asian meatball lettuce wraps immediately!

These Asian meatball lettuce wraps are flavorful, nutritious, and perfect for a light meal or appetizer. They can be easily customized with your favorite toppings and sauces, making them a versatile dish for any occasion. Adjust the spiciness of the sauce according to your taste preferences for a personalized touch!

Mushroom Pate Crostini

Ingredients:

For the Mushroom Pâté:

- 1 tablespoon olive oil
- 1 tablespoon unsalted butter
- 1/2 onion, finely chopped
- 2 cloves garlic, minced
- 1 pound mushrooms (such as cremini or button), finely chopped
- 1/4 cup dry white wine (optional)
- 2 tablespoons chopped fresh thyme (or 1 tablespoon dried thyme)
- Salt and pepper, to taste
- 1/4 cup cream cheese or mascarpone cheese
- 1/4 cup grated Parmesan cheese

For the Crostini:

- 1 French baguette, sliced into 1/2 inch thick rounds
- Olive oil, for brushing
- Salt and pepper, to taste
- Fresh parsley or thyme leaves, for garnish

Instructions:

1. Make the Mushroom Pâté:
    - Heat olive oil and butter in a large skillet over medium heat. Add chopped onion and sauté until translucent, about 3-4 minutes.
    - Add minced garlic and cook for another 1-2 minutes until fragrant.
    - Stir in chopped mushrooms and cook until they release their liquid and become tender, about 8-10 minutes.
    - If using, add dry white wine to deglaze the pan, scraping up any browned bits from the bottom. Cook until most of the liquid has evaporated.
    - Season with chopped fresh thyme (or dried thyme), salt, and pepper to taste. Remove from heat and let cool slightly.
    - Transfer the mushroom mixture to a food processor. Add cream cheese or mascarpone cheese and grated Parmesan cheese. Pulse until smooth and creamy. Adjust seasoning if needed.
2. Prepare the Crostini:
    - Preheat the oven to 375°F (190°C). Arrange baguette slices on a baking sheet in a single layer.
    - Brush both sides of each slice lightly with olive oil. Season with salt and pepper.
    - Bake in the preheated oven for 8-10 minutes, flipping halfway through, until golden brown and crispy. Remove from the oven and let cool slightly.

3. Assemble the Mushroom Pâté Crostini:
    - Spread a generous amount of mushroom pâté onto each toasted baguette slice.
    - Garnish with fresh parsley or thyme leaves for added freshness and flavor.
4. Serve:
    - Arrange the mushroom pâté crostini on a serving platter and serve immediately. Enjoy the creamy mushroom goodness paired with crispy bread!

These mushroom pâté crostini are perfect for parties, gatherings, or as an elegant appetizer before a meal. The mushroom pâté can be made ahead of time and refrigerated until ready to use. Warm slightly before spreading onto the crostini for serving. Adjust the consistency of the pâté by adding more cream cheese or mascarpone if desired.

Mini Beef Empanadas

Ingredients:

For the Dough:

- 2 cups all-purpose flour
- 1/2 teaspoon salt
- 1/2 cup unsalted butter, cold and cut into cubes
- 1/2 cup cold water

For the Filling:

- 1 tablespoon olive oil
- 1/2 onion, finely chopped
- 2 cloves garlic, minced
- 1/2 pound ground beef
- 1/2 teaspoon ground cumin
- 1/2 teaspoon paprika
- Salt and pepper, to taste
- 1/4 cup chopped green olives (optional)
- 1/4 cup raisins (optional)
- 2 hard-boiled eggs, chopped (optional)

For Assembly:

- 1 egg, beaten (for egg wash)
- Cooking spray or vegetable oil, for greasing

Instructions:

1. Make the Dough:
    - In a large bowl, whisk together the flour and salt. Add the cold cubed butter and use your fingers or a pastry cutter to cut the butter into the flour until the mixture resembles coarse crumbs.
    - Gradually add cold water, a little at a time, mixing until the dough comes together and forms a ball. You may not need to use all of the water. Wrap the dough in plastic wrap and refrigerate for at least 30 minutes.
2. Prepare the Filling:
    - In a skillet, heat olive oil over medium heat. Add chopped onions and sauté until translucent, about 3-4 minutes. Add minced garlic and cook for another minute until fragrant.
    - Add ground beef to the skillet and cook until browned and cooked through, breaking it up with a spoon as it cooks.

- Stir in ground cumin, paprika, salt, and pepper. Cook for another 1-2 minutes to allow the flavors to meld.
- Remove from heat and stir in chopped green olives, raisins, and chopped hard-boiled eggs if using. Let the filling cool completely.

3. Assemble the Empanadas:
   - Preheat the oven to 375°F (190°C). Line a baking sheet with parchment paper and lightly grease with cooking spray or vegetable oil.
   - On a lightly floured surface, roll out the chilled dough to about 1/8 inch thickness. Use a round cookie cutter or the rim of a glass (approximately 3-4 inches in diameter) to cut out circles of dough.
   - Place a spoonful of the cooled beef filling in the center of each dough circle. Fold the dough over the filling to create a half-moon shape. Press the edges together with your fingers or use a fork to crimp and seal the edges.
   - Place the assembled mini empanadas on the prepared baking sheet. Brush the tops with beaten egg for a shiny finish.

4. Bake the Empanadas:
   - Bake in the preheated oven for 20-25 minutes, or until the empanadas are golden brown and crispy.

5. Serve:
   - Remove from the oven and let cool slightly before serving. Mini beef empanadas can be served warm or at room temperature. Enjoy as a delicious appetizer or snack!

These mini beef empanadas can be customized with various fillings and are great for parties or gatherings. You can also make a large batch and freeze them before baking for convenient reheating later. Adjust the seasoning and add extra ingredients like olives, raisins, or hard-boiled eggs according to your taste preferences.

Pigs in a Blanket

Ingredients:

- 1 package (8 count) refrigerated crescent roll dough (or puff pastry, if preferred)
- 8 cocktail sausages or hot dogs
- Optional: 1/2 cup shredded cheese (cheddar or your choice)
- Optional: Mustard or dipping sauces of your choice

Instructions:

1. Preheat the Oven:
    - Preheat your oven according to the package instructions of the crescent roll dough (typically around 375°F or 190°C).
2. Prepare the Dough:
    - If using crescent roll dough, unroll the dough and separate into triangles along the perforations. If using puff pastry, roll it out slightly on a floured surface and cut into strips.
3. Assemble the Pigs in a Blanket:
    - If using cheese, sprinkle a small amount (about 1 tablespoon) onto each dough triangle or strip.
    - Place one cocktail sausage or hot dog on the wider end of each triangle or strip of dough.
    - Roll the dough around the sausage/hot dog, starting from the wider end and tucking the sides as you go, until the sausage/hot dog is completely wrapped.
4. Arrange on Baking Sheet:
    - Place the wrapped pigs in a blanket seam side down on a baking sheet lined with parchment paper or lightly greased.
5. Bake:
    - Bake in the preheated oven for 12-15 minutes, or until the dough is golden brown and cooked through.
6. Serve:
    - Remove from the oven and let cool slightly. Serve pigs in a blanket warm with mustard or your favorite dipping sauces.
7. Enjoy:
    - Pigs in a blanket are best served fresh out of the oven when the dough is crispy and the sausages/hot dogs are hot. They are perfect for parties, game days, or as a fun snack any time!

This recipe is versatile, and you can customize it by adding cheese inside the blanket or experimenting with different types of sausages or dipping sauces. It's a crowd-pleasing appetizer that is quick and easy to prepare.

Fried Ravioli with Marinara Sauce

Ingredients:

For the Fried Ravioli:

- 1 package (about 20 ounces) refrigerated cheese ravioli (or any filling of your choice)
- 2 cups Italian-style breadcrumbs
- 1/2 cup grated Parmesan cheese
- 2 large eggs
- 2 tablespoons milk
- Salt and pepper, to taste
- Cooking oil (vegetable or canola), for frying

For the Marinara Dipping Sauce:

- 1 can (15 ounces) crushed tomatoes
- 2 cloves garlic, minced
- 1 tablespoon olive oil
- 1 teaspoon dried oregano
- 1 teaspoon dried basil
- Salt and pepper, to taste
- Pinch of sugar (optional, to balance acidity)

Instructions:

1. Prepare the Marinara Sauce:
    - Heat olive oil in a saucepan over medium heat. Add minced garlic and sauté until fragrant, about 1 minute.
    - Stir in crushed tomatoes, dried oregano, dried basil, salt, pepper, and a pinch of sugar (if using). Bring to a simmer and cook for 15-20 minutes, stirring occasionally, until the sauce thickens slightly. Adjust seasoning to taste. Keep warm while preparing the fried ravioli.
2. Prepare the Fried Ravioli:
    - Cook the ravioli according to the package instructions until they are al dente. Drain and let cool slightly.
    - In a shallow bowl, whisk together eggs and milk. In another shallow bowl, combine Italian-style breadcrumbs, grated Parmesan cheese, salt, and pepper.
    - Dip each cooked ravioli in the egg mixture, allowing excess to drip off, then coat evenly with the breadcrumb mixture. Press gently to adhere the breadcrumbs.
3. Fry the Ravioli:
    - In a large skillet, heat about 1/2 inch of cooking oil over medium-high heat until hot (around 350°F or 175°C).

- Carefully place the breaded ravioli in the hot oil in batches, making sure not to overcrowd the skillet. Fry for 2-3 minutes per side, or until golden brown and crispy. Use tongs to carefully flip them halfway through cooking.
- Remove the fried ravioli with a slotted spoon and transfer to a plate lined with paper towels to drain excess oil.

4. Serve:
    - Arrange the fried ravioli on a serving platter and serve warm with the marinara dipping sauce on the side.
5. Enjoy:
    - Fried ravioli with marinara sauce is best enjoyed immediately while the ravioli are crispy and the marinara sauce is warm and flavorful. Serve as an appetizer or a delicious snack for any occasion!

This recipe for fried ravioli with marinara sauce is sure to be a hit with its crispy texture and comforting flavors. You can also garnish the dish with freshly grated Parmesan cheese and chopped fresh parsley for extra freshness and presentation.

Teriyaki Chicken Skewers

Ingredients:

For the Teriyaki Marinade:

- 1/2 cup soy sauce
- 1/4 cup water
- 1/4 cup brown sugar
- 2 tablespoons honey
- 2 tablespoons rice vinegar
- 2 cloves garlic, minced
- 1 tablespoon grated fresh ginger
- 1 tablespoon cornstarch (optional, for thickening)
- Optional: 1 teaspoon sesame seeds, for garnish

For the Chicken Skewers:

- 1.5 pounds boneless, skinless chicken breasts or thighs, cut into 1-inch cubes
- Wooden skewers, soaked in water for at least 30 minutes to prevent burning
- Cooking oil, for grilling
- Optional: Sliced green onions and sesame seeds, for garnish

Instructions:

1. Make the Teriyaki Marinade:
   - In a small saucepan, combine soy sauce, water, brown sugar, honey, rice vinegar, minced garlic, and grated ginger. Bring to a simmer over medium heat, stirring occasionally until the sugar has dissolved.
   - If desired, mix cornstarch with 1-2 tablespoons of water to create a slurry, then stir it into the simmering sauce. Cook for an additional 1-2 minutes until the sauce thickens slightly. Remove from heat and let cool to room temperature.
2. Marinate the Chicken:
   - Place the chicken cubes in a bowl or resealable plastic bag. Pour about half of the teriyaki marinade over the chicken, reserving the rest for basting and serving later. Ensure the chicken is well-coated. Marinate in the refrigerator for at least 30 minutes, or up to 2 hours for best flavor.
3. Skewer the Chicken:
   - Preheat the grill or grill pan over medium-high heat. Thread the marinated chicken pieces onto the soaked wooden skewers, leaving a little space between each piece.
4. Grill the Skewers:
   - Brush the grill lightly with cooking oil to prevent sticking. Place the skewers on the grill and cook for 6-8 minutes per side, or until the chicken is fully cooked

through and has nice grill marks. Baste with the reserved teriyaki sauce during grilling.
5. Serve:
    - Remove the teriyaki chicken skewers from the grill and transfer them to a serving platter. Sprinkle with sliced green onions and sesame seeds for garnish, if desired.
6. Enjoy:
    - Serve the teriyaki chicken skewers hot, accompanied by remaining teriyaki sauce for dipping or drizzling. They are perfect as an appetizer or main dish, and pair well with steamed rice and vegetables.

These teriyaki chicken skewers are a crowd-pleasing dish with their sweet and savory flavor profile. Customize the recipe by adding pineapple chunks or bell peppers to the skewers for additional flavor and color. Adjust the sweetness or saltiness of the teriyaki sauce to suit your taste preferences for a personalized touch!

Bacon-Wrapped Jalapeño Poppers

Ingredients:

- 12 fresh jalapeño peppers
- 8 ounces cream cheese, softened
- 1/2 cup shredded cheddar cheese (or cheese of your choice)
- 1/2 teaspoon garlic powder
- Salt and pepper, to taste
- 12 slices of bacon, cut in half crosswise
- Toothpicks or skewers (if needed)

Instructions:

1. Prepare the Jalapeños:
   - Preheat your oven to 375°F (190°C). Line a baking sheet with parchment paper or aluminum foil for easy cleanup.
   - Cut the jalapeños in half lengthwise and remove the seeds and membranes. Wear gloves or wash your hands thoroughly afterward to avoid irritation from the jalapeño seeds.
2. Make the Filling:
   - In a mixing bowl, combine softened cream cheese, shredded cheddar cheese, garlic powder, salt, and pepper. Mix until smooth and well combined.
3. Fill the Jalapeños:
   - Spoon the cheese mixture evenly into each jalapeño half, pressing gently to fill any cavities.
4. Wrap with Bacon:
   - Wrap each stuffed jalapeño half with a half slice of bacon, securing it with a toothpick or skewer if necessary. Make sure the bacon ends are underneath the jalapeño to keep them from unraveling during baking.
5. Bake the Poppers:
   - Arrange the bacon-wrapped jalapeño poppers on the prepared baking sheet, spaced apart.
   - Bake in the preheated oven for 20-25 minutes, or until the bacon is crispy and cooked to your desired doneness.
6. Serve:
   - Remove the bacon-wrapped jalapeño poppers from the oven and let them cool slightly before serving. Arrange them on a serving platter and enjoy them warm.
7. Optional: Grill Method
   - Alternatively, you can grill the bacon-wrapped jalapeño poppers on a preheated grill over medium heat. Grill for about 10-15 minutes, turning occasionally, until the bacon is crispy and the jalapeños are tender.
8. Enjoy:

- Bacon-wrapped jalapeño poppers are best served warm and can be enjoyed on their own or with dipping sauces such as ranch dressing or sour cream. They are perfect for parties, game days, or any occasion where you want a spicy and savory appetizer!

Feel free to adjust the filling ingredients to your liking, such as adding diced onions, garlic, or herbs for additional flavor. These bacon-wrapped jalapeño poppers are sure to be a hit with their irresistible combination of spicy, creamy, and crispy textures.

Tuna Tartare on Crispy Wontons

Ingredients:

For the Tuna Tartare:

- 1/2 pound sushi-grade tuna, diced into small cubes
- 2 tablespoons soy sauce
- 1 tablespoon sesame oil
- 1 tablespoon rice vinegar
- 1 teaspoon honey
- 1 teaspoon fresh ginger, grated
- 1 teaspoon Sriracha sauce (adjust to taste)
- 2 green onions, thinly sliced
- 1 tablespoon sesame seeds, toasted
- Salt and pepper, to taste

For the Crispy Wontons:

- 12 wonton wrappers
- Cooking oil (vegetable or canola), for frying
- Salt, to taste

For Garnish (optional):

- Thinly sliced cucumber
- Avocado slices
- Microgreens or sprouts
- Additional sesame seeds
- Soy sauce or ponzu sauce, for drizzling

Instructions:

1. Prepare the Tuna Tartare:
   - In a mixing bowl, combine diced tuna with soy sauce, sesame oil, rice vinegar, honey, grated ginger, Sriracha sauce, green onions, and toasted sesame seeds. Season with salt and pepper to taste. Gently toss until well combined. Cover and refrigerate while you prepare the crispy wontons.
2. Make the Crispy Wontons:
   - Cut each wonton wrapper into quarters to create smaller triangles.
   - Heat about 1 inch of cooking oil in a skillet or frying pan over medium-high heat until hot (around 350°F or 175°C).
   - Carefully add a few wonton triangles at a time to the hot oil, frying for about 1-2 minutes per side until golden brown and crispy. Use tongs to flip them halfway through cooking if needed.

- Remove the crispy wontons from the oil and drain on paper towels to remove excess oil. Sprinkle lightly with salt while they are still hot. Repeat until all wonton triangles are fried.
3. Assemble the Tuna Tartare on Crispy Wontons:
    - Arrange the crispy wontons on a serving platter or individual plates.
    - Spoon a small amount of the chilled tuna tartare mixture onto each crispy wonton.
4. Garnish (optional):
    - Garnish each tuna tartare on crispy wonton with thinly sliced cucumber, avocado slices, microgreens or sprouts, and additional toasted sesame seeds if desired.
5. Serve:
    - Drizzle each tuna tartare on crispy wonton with soy sauce or ponzu sauce just before serving. Enjoy immediately as a flavorful and refreshing appetizer!

This tuna tartare on crispy wontons recipe is perfect for special occasions or gatherings, offering a balance of textures and flavors with the fresh tuna, crispy wontons, and Asian-inspired marinade. Adjust the spiciness of the Sriracha sauce to your preference and customize the garnishes to suit your taste. It's sure to impress your guests with its visual appeal and delicious taste!

Mini Reuben Sandwiches

Ingredients:

- Cocktail rye bread slices (or mini rye bread slices)
- Thinly sliced corned beef
- Swiss cheese slices, cut into small squares
- Sauerkraut, drained
- Russian dressing (store-bought or homemade)
- Butter or margarine, softened

Instructions:

1. Prepare the Bread:
    - Preheat a non-stick skillet or griddle over medium heat.
    - Lightly butter one side of each slice of cocktail rye bread.
2. Assemble the Mini Reuben Sandwiches:
    - Place the bread slices butter-side down on the skillet or griddle.
    - On each slice of bread, layer a piece of Swiss cheese, followed by a small amount of drained sauerkraut, and finally a slice of corned beef.
    - Spread Russian dressing on the inside of another slice of bread and place it on top of the corned beef, butter-side up.
3. Grill the Sandwiches:
    - Grill the mini Reuben sandwiches for about 2-3 minutes on each side, or until the bread is golden brown and the cheese is melted.
    - Press down lightly with a spatula while grilling to ensure the sandwich holds together and the cheese melts evenly.
4. Serve:
    - Remove the mini Reuben sandwiches from the skillet or griddle and let them cool slightly.
    - Optionally, cut each sandwich into halves or quarters for bite-sized portions.
5. Enjoy:
    - Serve the mini Reuben sandwiches warm as a delicious appetizer or party snack. They pair well with pickles, coleslaw, or a side of potato chips.

These mini Reuben sandwiches are perfect for parties, gatherings, or even as a fun twist on lunch. The combination of savory corned beef, tangy sauerkraut, melty Swiss cheese, and creamy Russian dressing on crispy rye bread is sure to be a hit with guests! Adjust the ingredient quantities to make as many mini sandwiches as needed for your event.

Spicy Thai Chicken Satay

Ingredients:

For the Chicken Satay:

- 1 pound chicken breast or thighs, cut into thin strips or cubes
- 1/4 cup coconut milk
- 2 tablespoons soy sauce
- 2 tablespoons fish sauce
- 1 tablespoon brown sugar
- 2 cloves garlic, minced
- 1 tablespoon curry powder
- 1 tablespoon sriracha sauce (adjust to taste)
- 1 tablespoon lime juice
- 1 tablespoon vegetable oil
- Bamboo skewers, soaked in water for at least 30 minutes

For the Spicy Peanut Dipping Sauce:

- 1/2 cup creamy peanut butter
- 1/4 cup coconut milk
- 2 tablespoons soy sauce
- 1 tablespoon brown sugar
- 1 tablespoon lime juice
- 1 teaspoon sriracha sauce (adjust to taste)
- 1 clove garlic, minced
- Water (as needed to adjust consistency)

For Garnish (optional):

- Chopped fresh cilantro
- Crushed peanuts
- Lime wedges

Instructions:

1. Marinate the Chicken:
    - In a bowl, combine coconut milk, soy sauce, fish sauce, brown sugar, minced garlic, curry powder, sriracha sauce, lime juice, and vegetable oil. Mix well to combine.
    - Add the chicken strips or cubes to the marinade, making sure they are evenly coated. Cover and refrigerate for at least 1 hour, or overnight for best flavor.
2. Make the Spicy Peanut Dipping Sauce:

- In a small saucepan over low heat, combine peanut butter, coconut milk, soy sauce, brown sugar, lime juice, sriracha sauce, and minced garlic.
- Stir continuously until the mixture is smooth and heated through. If the sauce is too thick, gradually add water, a tablespoon at a time, until you reach your desired consistency. Remove from heat and set aside.

3. Prepare the Chicken Satay:
    - Preheat the grill or grill pan over medium-high heat. Thread the marinated chicken onto soaked bamboo skewers, dividing evenly.
    - Grill the chicken satay skewers for 3-4 minutes on each side, or until the chicken is cooked through and has nice grill marks. Baste with any remaining marinade while grilling.
4. Serve:
    - Arrange the grilled spicy Thai chicken satay skewers on a serving platter.
    - Serve the chicken satay hot with the spicy peanut dipping sauce on the side.
5. Garnish (optional):
    - Garnish with chopped fresh cilantro, crushed peanuts, and lime wedges for squeezing over the chicken satay.
6. Enjoy:
    - Enjoy the spicy Thai chicken satay as an appetizer or main dish, accompanied by steamed rice or a refreshing salad. The creamy and spicy peanut dipping sauce complements the tender grilled chicken perfectly!

This recipe allows you to adjust the level of spiciness by varying the amount of sriracha sauce in both the marinade and the peanut dipping sauce. It's a delicious and satisfying dish that captures the vibrant flavors of Thai cuisine, perfect for any occasion.

Crab Stuffed Avocado

Ingredients:

- 2 ripe avocados
- 8 ounces lump crab meat, drained and picked over for shells
- 1/4 cup mayonnaise
- 1 tablespoon fresh lemon juice
- 1/2 teaspoon Dijon mustard
- 1 green onion, finely chopped
- 1/2 celery stalk, finely chopped
- Salt and pepper, to taste
- Optional: Old Bay seasoning, paprika, or cayenne pepper for extra flavor
- Fresh parsley or cilantro, chopped (for garnish)

Instructions:

1. Prepare the Avocados:
    - Cut the avocados in half lengthwise and remove the pits. Scoop out a little bit of flesh from each avocado half to create a larger cavity for the filling.
2. Make the Crab Salad Filling:
    - In a mixing bowl, combine lump crab meat, mayonnaise, fresh lemon juice, Dijon mustard, chopped green onion, and chopped celery. Season with salt, pepper, and optional spices to taste. Gently mix until well combined.
3. Stuff the Avocados:
    - Spoon the crab salad filling into the cavities of each avocado half, dividing evenly.
4. Garnish and Serve:
    - Sprinkle chopped parsley or cilantro over the stuffed avocados for garnish.
    - Serve immediately as an appetizer or light meal. You can also chill the stuffed avocados in the refrigerator for about 30 minutes before serving for a refreshing touch.
5. Variations:
    - For added crunch and flavor, you can mix in diced bell peppers or cucumber into the crab salad filling.
    - Drizzle a little extra lemon juice over the stuffed avocados before serving to enhance the freshness.
    - If you prefer a spicier kick, add a pinch of cayenne pepper or a dash of hot sauce to the crab salad filling.

This crab stuffed avocado recipe is simple yet elegant, highlighting the natural creaminess of avocado and the sweet, delicate flavor of lump crab meat. It's perfect for entertaining guests or enjoying as a light and refreshing meal. Adjust the seasoning and ingredients according to your taste preferences for a personalized touch!

Mediterranean Phyllo Cups

Ingredients:

- 1 package (about 15 sheets) phyllo dough, thawed if frozen
- 1/2 cup (1 stick) unsalted butter, melted
- 1 cup crumbled feta cheese
- 1/2 cup sun-dried tomatoes, chopped
- 1/2 cup Kalamata olives, chopped
- 1/4 cup fresh parsley, finely chopped
- 1/4 cup fresh basil, finely chopped
- 1/4 cup pine nuts, toasted (optional)
- Salt and pepper, to taste

Instructions:

1. Prepare the Phyllo Cups:
    - Preheat your oven to 350°F (175°C). Lightly grease a mini muffin tin with butter or cooking spray.
    - Lay one sheet of phyllo dough on a clean work surface and brush it with melted butter using a pastry brush. Layer another sheet of phyllo on top and brush with butter. Repeat until you have 5-6 layers of phyllo dough.
    - Cut the layered phyllo dough into squares (about 3x3 inches). Press each square gently into the prepared mini muffin tin, creating little cups.
2. Bake the Phyllo Cups:
    - Bake the phyllo cups in the preheated oven for 8-10 minutes, or until golden brown and crispy. Keep an eye on them as they can brown quickly.
    - Remove from the oven and let cool in the muffin tin for a few minutes, then carefully transfer the phyllo cups to a wire rack to cool completely.
3. Prepare the Filling:
    - In a mixing bowl, combine crumbled feta cheese, chopped sun-dried tomatoes, chopped Kalamata olives, finely chopped parsley, finely chopped basil, and toasted pine nuts (if using). Season with salt and pepper to taste.
4. Assemble the Mediterranean Phyllo Cups:
    - Spoon the Mediterranean filling into each cooled phyllo cup, dividing evenly among them.
5. Serve:
    - Arrange the filled Mediterranean phyllo cups on a serving platter.
    - Serve immediately as an appetizer or snack. They can be served warm or at room temperature.
6. Optional Garnish:
    - Garnish each Mediterranean phyllo cup with additional chopped herbs or a drizzle of balsamic glaze for extra flavor and presentation.

These Mediterranean phyllo cups are versatile and can be customized with your favorite Mediterranean ingredients such as artichoke hearts, roasted red peppers, or capers. They are perfect for parties, gatherings, or any occasion where you want to impress with a flavorful and elegant appetizer!

Bacon and Cheese Stuffed Mushrooms

Ingredients:

- 12 large mushrooms, such as cremini or button mushrooms
- 6 slices bacon, cooked until crispy and crumbled
- 1/2 cup shredded mozzarella cheese (or cheese of your choice)
- 1/4 cup grated Parmesan cheese
- 1/4 cup cream cheese, softened
- 2 tablespoons chopped fresh parsley
- 2 cloves garlic, minced
- Salt and pepper, to taste
- Cooking spray or olive oil, for greasing

Instructions:

1. Prepare the Mushrooms:
   - Preheat your oven to 375°F (190°C). Lightly grease a baking dish or a baking sheet with cooking spray or olive oil.
   - Clean the mushrooms with a damp cloth or paper towel to remove any dirt. Remove the stems from the mushrooms and finely chop them. Set aside.
2. Make the Filling:
   - In a mixing bowl, combine crumbled bacon, shredded mozzarella cheese, grated Parmesan cheese, softened cream cheese, chopped parsley, minced garlic, and the chopped mushroom stems. Season with salt and pepper to taste. Mix until well combined.
3. Stuff the Mushrooms:
   - Spoon the bacon and cheese mixture into each mushroom cap, pressing gently to fill and mound the filling.
4. Bake the Stuffed Mushrooms:
   - Place the stuffed mushrooms in the prepared baking dish or baking sheet.
   - Bake in the preheated oven for 18-20 minutes, or until the mushrooms are tender and the filling is golden and bubbly.
5. Serve:
   - Remove from the oven and let cool slightly before serving.
   - Arrange the bacon and cheese stuffed mushrooms on a serving platter and garnish with additional chopped parsley if desired.
6. Enjoy:
   - Serve the bacon and cheese stuffed mushrooms warm as a delicious appetizer or snack. They are perfect for parties, game days, or any gathering where you want to impress with a flavorful and comforting dish!

These bacon and cheese stuffed mushrooms are sure to be a hit with their combination of savory bacon, creamy cheeses, and aromatic garlic and parsley. You can customize the recipe by adding a pinch of red pepper flakes for a spicy kick or substituting different types of cheese according to your preference. Enjoy these delicious stuffed mushrooms straight out of the oven for the best experience!

Artichoke Spinach Puff Pastry Pinwheels

Ingredients:

- 1 sheet of puff pastry, thawed according to package instructions
- 1 cup frozen spinach, thawed and excess water squeezed out
- 1 cup canned artichoke hearts, drained and chopped
- 1/2 cup shredded mozzarella cheese
- 1/4 cup grated Parmesan cheese
- 1/4 cup mayonnaise
- 1 clove garlic, minced
- 1/2 teaspoon dried oregano
- Salt and pepper, to taste
- 1 egg, beaten (for egg wash)

Instructions:

1. Preheat Oven:
    - Preheat your oven to 400°F (200°C). Line a baking sheet with parchment paper.
2. Prepare Filling:
    - In a mixing bowl, combine thawed spinach, chopped artichoke hearts, shredded mozzarella cheese, grated Parmesan cheese, mayonnaise, minced garlic, dried oregano, salt, and pepper. Mix until well combined.
3. Assemble Pinwheels:
    - Roll out the thawed puff pastry sheet on a lightly floured surface into a rectangle about 12x10 inches.
    - Spread the spinach and artichoke mixture evenly over the puff pastry, leaving a small border around the edges.
4. Roll and Slice:
    - Starting from one of the long sides, tightly roll the puff pastry sheet into a log.
    - Using a sharp knife, slice the log into 1/2-inch thick slices. You should get about 12 slices.
5. Bake:
    - Place the pinwheels cut-side down on the prepared baking sheet, spacing them a little apart.
    - Brush the tops of the pinwheels with beaten egg for a golden finish.
6. Bake:
    - Bake in the preheated oven for 15-18 minutes, or until the puff pastry is golden brown and puffed up.
7. Serve:
    - Remove from the oven and let cool slightly before serving.
    - Arrange the artichoke spinach puff pastry pinwheels on a serving platter and serve warm.
8. Optional Garnish:

- Garnish with additional grated Parmesan cheese or chopped fresh herbs before serving if desired.

These artichoke spinach puff pastry pinwheels are a crowd-pleasing appetizer with their flaky pastry and flavorful filling. They can be enjoyed warm or at room temperature, making them perfect for any occasion. Customize the recipe by adding a pinch of red pepper flakes for a hint of spice or substituting different cheeses according to your preference. Enjoy these delicious pinwheels as a tasty appetizer that's sure to impress!

Caprese Salad Skewers

Ingredients:

- Cherry or grape tomatoes
- Fresh mozzarella balls (bocconcini or ciliegine)
- Fresh basil leaves
- Balsamic glaze or balsamic reduction
- Extra virgin olive oil
- Salt and pepper, to taste
- Toothpicks or small skewers

Instructions:

1. Prepare the Ingredients:
   - If using large mozzarella balls (bocconcini), cut them into smaller, bite-sized pieces.
   - Wash and dry the cherry or grape tomatoes. Pick basil leaves and set aside.
2. Assemble the Skewers:
   - Thread one cherry tomato onto a toothpick or skewer, followed by a basil leaf (folded or whole), and then a mozzarella ball.
   - Repeat this pattern for each skewer until all ingredients are used.
3. Season the Skewers:
   - Arrange the Caprese salad skewers on a serving platter.
   - Drizzle lightly with extra virgin olive oil and balsamic glaze or reduction.
   - Season with salt and pepper to taste.
4. Serve:
   - Serve the Caprese salad skewers immediately as a colorful and flavorful appetizer.
5. Optional Variations:
   - Instead of balsamic glaze, you can use a drizzle of balsamic vinegar mixed with a touch of honey for sweetness.
   - Add a sprinkle of dried oregano or freshly cracked black pepper for extra flavor.
   - If serving for a party or gathering, you can prepare the skewers ahead of time and refrigerate them until ready to serve. Just drizzle with olive oil and balsamic glaze right before serving to keep them fresh.

Caprese salad skewers are not only visually appealing but also incredibly tasty with the combination of fresh tomatoes, creamy mozzarella, and aromatic basil. They are perfect for any occasion, from casual gatherings to formal events, and are sure to be a hit with guests!

Baked Buffalo Chicken Dip

Ingredients:

- 2 cups cooked chicken breast, shredded or diced (about 2 medium-sized chicken breasts)
- 1/2 cup buffalo sauce (such as Frank's RedHot or your favorite brand)
- 1/2 cup ranch or blue cheese dressing
- 1/2 cup shredded mozzarella cheese
- 1/2 cup shredded cheddar cheese
- 1/4 cup cream cheese, softened
- 1/4 cup sour cream
- 1/4 cup mayonnaise
- 1 teaspoon garlic powder
- 1/2 teaspoon onion powder
- Salt and pepper, to taste
- Chopped green onions or fresh cilantro, for garnish (optional)
- Tortilla chips, crackers, or vegetable sticks, for serving

Instructions:

1. Preheat the Oven:
    - Preheat your oven to 375°F (190°C). Lightly grease a baking dish or oven-safe skillet with cooking spray or butter.
2. Prepare the Chicken:
    - Cook and shred or dice the chicken breasts. You can boil, bake, or use leftover rotisserie chicken for this recipe.
3. Make the Dip:
    - In a large mixing bowl, combine the shredded chicken, buffalo sauce, ranch or blue cheese dressing, shredded mozzarella cheese, shredded cheddar cheese, cream cheese, sour cream, mayonnaise, garlic powder, onion powder, salt, and pepper. Mix until well combined.
4. Bake the Dip:
    - Transfer the mixture to the prepared baking dish or skillet, spreading it out evenly.
    - Bake in the preheated oven for 20-25 minutes, or until the dip is hot and bubbly and the cheese is melted and lightly browned on top.
5. Serve:
    - Remove from the oven and let the dip cool slightly.
    - Garnish with chopped green onions or fresh cilantro, if desired.
    - Serve the Baked Buffalo Chicken Dip warm with tortilla chips, crackers, or vegetable sticks for dipping.
6. Enjoy:
    - Enjoy this delicious dip as a game day snack, party appetizer, or anytime you crave a spicy and creamy treat!

This Baked Buffalo Chicken Dip is creamy, cheesy, and has just the right amount of buffalo sauce kick. It's sure to be a hit at any gathering or party, and you can adjust the spice level to your preference by adding more or less buffalo sauce. Serve it alongside your favorite dippers for a satisfying and flavorful appetizer experience!

Chicken and Pineapple Skewers

Ingredients:

- 1 pound chicken breast or thighs, cut into 1-inch cubes
- 1 small pineapple, peeled, cored, and cut into 1-inch chunks
- 1 red bell pepper, cut into 1-inch pieces (optional)
- 1 green bell pepper, cut into 1-inch pieces (optional)
- Wooden or metal skewers

Marinade:

- 1/4 cup soy sauce
- 2 tablespoons honey
- 2 tablespoons olive oil
- 2 cloves garlic, minced
- 1 teaspoon ground ginger
- 1/2 teaspoon black pepper
- 1 tablespoon fresh lime juice (optional)
- Fresh cilantro or parsley, chopped (for garnish)

Instructions:

1. Prepare the Marinade:
   - In a small bowl, whisk together soy sauce, honey, olive oil, minced garlic, ground ginger, black pepper, and fresh lime juice (if using).
2. Marinate the Chicken:
   - Place the chicken cubes in a resealable plastic bag or shallow dish. Pour the marinade over the chicken, making sure it is evenly coated. Seal the bag or cover the dish and refrigerate for at least 30 minutes, or up to 2 hours for maximum flavor.
3. Assemble the Skewers:
   - If using wooden skewers, soak them in water for at least 30 minutes to prevent burning during grilling.
   - Preheat the grill to medium-high heat.
   - Thread the marinated chicken, pineapple chunks, and bell pepper pieces (if using) alternately onto the skewers.
4. Grill the Skewers:
   - Place the assembled skewers on the preheated grill. Grill for about 8-10 minutes, turning occasionally, until the chicken is cooked through and the pineapple is caramelized and slightly charred.
5. Serve:
   - Remove the skewers from the grill and transfer them to a serving platter.
   - Sprinkle with chopped cilantro or parsley for garnish.
6. Enjoy:
   - Serve the chicken and pineapple skewers hot as a main dish or appetizer. They pair well with rice, quinoa, or a fresh salad.

These chicken and pineapple skewers are perfect for summer grilling or any time you want a quick and flavorful meal. The marinade adds depth of flavor to the chicken, while the grilled pineapple adds a delicious sweetness. Customize the skewers by adding your favorite vegetables or adjusting the seasoning to your taste.

Greek Meatballs with Tzatziki Sauce

Ingredients:

For the Greek Meatballs (Keftedes):

- 1 pound ground beef or lamb (or a mixture of both)
- 1/2 cup breadcrumbs
- 1/4 cup finely chopped onion
- 2 cloves garlic, minced
- 1/4 cup chopped fresh parsley
- 1 tablespoon chopped fresh mint (optional)
- 1 teaspoon dried oregano
- 1 teaspoon ground cumin
- 1 teaspoon ground coriander
- 1/2 teaspoon ground cinnamon
- Salt and pepper, to taste
- 1 egg
- Olive oil, for frying

For the Tzatziki Sauce:

- 1 cup Greek yogurt
- 1/2 cucumber, grated and excess liquid squeezed out
- 1 clove garlic, minced
- 1 tablespoon lemon juice
- 1 tablespoon chopped fresh dill (or 1 teaspoon dried dill)
- Salt and pepper, to taste

Instructions:

1. Make the Tzatziki Sauce:
    - In a bowl, combine Greek yogurt, grated cucumber, minced garlic, lemon juice, chopped dill, salt, and pepper. Mix well until smooth and creamy. Refrigerate the tzatziki sauce for at least 30 minutes to allow the flavors to meld.
2. Prepare the Greek Meatballs (Keftedes):
    - In a large mixing bowl, combine ground beef or lamb, breadcrumbs, finely chopped onion, minced garlic, chopped parsley, chopped mint (if using), dried oregano, ground cumin, ground coriander, ground cinnamon, salt, pepper, and egg. Mix until well combined.
    - Shape the mixture into small meatballs, about 1 inch in diameter.
3. Cook the Greek Meatballs:
    - Heat olive oil in a large skillet over medium heat.
    - Add the meatballs in batches, making sure not to overcrowd the pan. Cook for about 8-10 minutes, turning occasionally, until the meatballs are browned on all sides and cooked through.
    - Transfer the cooked meatballs to a plate lined with paper towels to absorb any excess oil.
4. Serve:

- Arrange the Greek meatballs on a serving platter.
        - Serve warm with the chilled tzatziki sauce on the side for dipping or drizzling over the meatballs.
5. Garnish (optional):
    - Garnish the Greek meatballs with additional chopped fresh parsley or mint before serving, if desired.
6. Enjoy:
    - Enjoy these Greek meatballs with tzatziki sauce as an appetizer, main dish served with rice or pita bread, or as part of a Mediterranean-inspired meal. They are flavorful, juicy, and perfect for sharing with friends and family!

This recipe captures the essence of Greek cuisine with its robust flavors and creamy tzatziki sauce. Adjust the seasoning and spices according to your taste preferences for a personalized touch.

Mini Lobster Rolls

Ingredients:

- 1 pound cooked lobster meat, chopped into bite-sized pieces
- 1/2 cup mayonnaise

- 2 tablespoons finely chopped celery
- 1 tablespoon finely chopped fresh chives (plus more for garnish)
- 1 tablespoon fresh lemon juice
- Salt and pepper, to taste
- Mini brioche rolls or dinner rolls
- Butter, for toasting the rolls
- Optional: Lettuce leaves or microgreens for garnish

Instructions:

1. Prepare the Lobster Salad:
   - In a mixing bowl, combine the chopped lobster meat, mayonnaise, finely chopped celery, finely chopped chives, and fresh lemon juice. Season with salt and pepper to taste. Mix gently until well combined.
2. Toast the Rolls:
   - Slice the mini brioche rolls or dinner rolls in half horizontally. Lightly butter the cut sides of the rolls.
   - Heat a skillet or griddle over medium heat. Place the rolls, cut side down, on the skillet and toast until golden brown and lightly crisp. This should take about 1-2 minutes.
3. Assemble the Mini Lobster Rolls:
   - Spoon a generous portion of the lobster salad into each toasted roll.
4. Garnish and Serve:
   - Garnish each mini lobster roll with additional chopped chives and a small lettuce leaf or microgreens, if desired.
   - Arrange the mini lobster rolls on a serving platter.
5. Enjoy:
   - Serve the mini lobster rolls immediately as an elegant appetizer or snack.

These mini lobster rolls are perfect for parties, brunches, or any special occasion where you want to impress your guests with a taste of gourmet seafood. The creamy lobster salad paired with buttery, toasted rolls creates a delightful combination that's sure to please everyone's palate. Adjust the seasoning and ingredients according to your preference, and enjoy these delicious bites with friends and family!

Sweet Potato Rounds with Goat Cheese

Ingredients:

- 2 medium sweet potatoes, peeled and sliced into 1/4-inch rounds
- Olive oil, for drizzling

- Salt and pepper, to taste
- 4 ounces soft goat cheese (chevre), crumbled
- Honey, for drizzling (optional)
- Fresh thyme leaves, for garnish (optional)

Instructions:

1. Preheat the Oven:
    - Preheat your oven to 400°F (200°C). Line a baking sheet with parchment paper or aluminum foil for easy cleanup.
2. Prepare the Sweet Potatoes:
    - Peel the sweet potatoes and slice them into rounds about 1/4-inch thick. Try to make them as uniform in thickness as possible for even cooking.
3. Season and Bake:
    - Arrange the sweet potato rounds on the prepared baking sheet in a single layer.
    - Drizzle olive oil over the sweet potato rounds and toss to coat them evenly. Season with salt and pepper to taste.
    - Bake in the preheated oven for 20-25 minutes, flipping halfway through, until the sweet potatoes are tender and lightly browned around the edges.
4. Assemble the Sweet Potato Rounds:
    - Remove the sweet potato rounds from the oven and let them cool slightly.
    - Top each sweet potato round with a crumble of goat cheese.
5. Serve:
    - Drizzle a little honey over each sweet potato round, if desired, for a touch of sweetness.
    - Garnish with fresh thyme leaves for additional flavor and presentation.
6. Enjoy:
    - Serve the sweet potato rounds with goat cheese warm as an appetizer or side dish.

These sweet potato rounds with goat cheese are a wonderful combination of sweet and savory flavors. They make a great addition to any gathering or holiday spread, and the creamy goat cheese complements the sweetness of the roasted sweet potatoes beautifully. Customize the dish by adding chopped nuts, a sprinkle of cinnamon, or a balsamic reduction drizzle for extra flair.

Teriyaki Beef Skewers

Ingredients:

- 1 pound beef sirloin or flank steak, cut into 1-inch cubes

- 1/2 cup soy sauce
- 1/4 cup mirin (Japanese sweet rice wine)
- 2 tablespoons brown sugar
- 2 cloves garlic, minced
- 1 teaspoon minced ginger
- 1 tablespoon sesame oil
- 2 tablespoons vegetable oil (for grilling)
- Wooden skewers, soaked in water for 30 minutes (if using)

Instructions:

1. Prepare the Marinade:
    - In a mixing bowl, whisk together soy sauce, mirin, brown sugar, minced garlic, minced ginger, and sesame oil until the sugar is dissolved and the marinade is well combined.
2. Marinate the Beef:
    - Place the beef cubes in a resealable plastic bag or shallow dish. Pour the teriyaki marinade over the beef, making sure it is evenly coated. Seal the bag or cover the dish and refrigerate for at least 30 minutes, or up to 2 hours for maximum flavor.
3. Assemble the Skewers:
    - Preheat your grill to medium-high heat or preheat your broiler.
    - Thread the marinated beef cubes onto the skewers, leaving a little space between each piece.
4. Grill or Broil the Skewers:
    - If grilling: Brush the grill grates with vegetable oil to prevent sticking. Place the skewers on the grill and cook for about 3-4 minutes per side, or until the beef is cooked to your desired doneness and has nice grill marks.
    - If broiling: Arrange the skewers on a broiler pan or baking sheet lined with aluminum foil. Place under the broiler and cook for about 3-4 minutes per side, or until the beef is cooked through and caramelized.
5. Serve:
    - Remove the teriyaki beef skewers from the grill or broiler and let them rest for a few minutes.
    - Serve the skewers hot, garnished with chopped green onions or sesame seeds if desired.
6. Enjoy:
    - Enjoy these delicious teriyaki beef skewers as a main dish with rice and vegetables, or as an appetizer for parties and gatherings.

These teriyaki beef skewers are flavorful and easy to prepare, making them a great choice for any occasion. The marinade adds a rich umami flavor to the beef, while grilling or broiling gives the meat a delicious caramelized exterior. Adjust the cooking time according to the thickness of your beef cubes and your preferred level of doneness.

Caramelized Onion and Gruyere Tartlets

Ingredients:

- 1 sheet frozen puff pastry, thawed according to package instructions
- 2 large onions, thinly sliced
- 2 tablespoons unsalted butter
- 1 tablespoon olive oil
- 1 teaspoon granulated sugar (optional, to aid caramelization)
- Salt and pepper, to taste
- 1 cup shredded Gruyere cheese (or Swiss cheese)
- Fresh thyme leaves, for garnish (optional)

Instructions:

1. Prepare the Puff Pastry:
   - Preheat your oven to 400°F (200°C). Line a baking sheet with parchment paper.
   - Roll out the thawed puff pastry sheet on a lightly floured surface. Using a round cookie cutter or a glass, cut out circles of puff pastry that fit into the cavities of a mini muffin tin.
   - Press the puff pastry circles gently into the mini muffin tin, forming small tartlet shells. Prick the bottom of each shell with a fork to prevent puffing.
2. Caramelize the Onions:
   - In a large skillet, heat the butter and olive oil over medium heat until the butter is melted.
   - Add the thinly sliced onions to the skillet. Cook, stirring occasionally, until the onions are softened and golden brown, about 20-25 minutes.
   - If desired, sprinkle a teaspoon of granulated sugar over the onions to aid caramelization and continue cooking until the onions are caramelized to your liking. Season with salt and pepper to taste.
3. Assemble the Tartlets:
   - Distribute the caramelized onions evenly among the puff pastry shells.
   - Top each tartlet with shredded Gruyere cheese.
4. Bake the Tartlets:
   - Place the mini muffin tin in the preheated oven and bake for 15-18 minutes, or until the puff pastry is golden brown and the cheese is melted and bubbly.
5. Garnish and Serve:
   - Remove the caramelized onion and Gruyere tartlets from the oven and let them cool slightly in the muffin tin.
   - Carefully remove the tartlets from the tin and transfer them to a serving platter.
   - Garnish with fresh thyme leaves, if desired, and serve warm as a delicious appetizer.

These caramelized onion and Gruyere tartlets are perfect for parties, gatherings, or as a tasty snack. The combination of sweet caramelized onions and nutty Gruyere cheese in buttery puff pastry shells creates a mouthwatering treat that will impress your guests. Enjoy these savory tartlets straight out of the oven for the best flavor and texture!

Cajun Shrimp Cocktail

Ingredients:

- 1 pound large shrimp, peeled and deveined
- Cajun seasoning (store-bought or homemade)

- 1 tablespoon olive oil
- Cocktail sauce (store-bought or homemade, for serving)
- Lemon wedges, for serving
- Fresh parsley or cilantro, chopped, for garnish (optional)

Cajun Seasoning (Homemade):

- 1 tablespoon paprika
- 1 teaspoon garlic powder
- 1 teaspoon onion powder
- 1 teaspoon dried oregano
- 1 teaspoon dried thyme
- 1/2 teaspoon cayenne pepper (adjust to taste)
- 1/2 teaspoon black pepper
- 1/2 teaspoon salt

Cocktail Sauce (Homemade):

- 1/2 cup ketchup
- 2 tablespoons prepared horseradish
- 1 tablespoon lemon juice
- 1 teaspoon Worcestershire sauce
- Hot sauce, to taste (optional)

Instructions:

1. Prepare the Cajun Shrimp:
   - In a bowl, toss the peeled and deveined shrimp with Cajun seasoning until evenly coated. Use about 2-3 tablespoons of Cajun seasoning, depending on your spice preference.
   - Heat olive oil in a large skillet over medium-high heat. Add the seasoned shrimp to the skillet and cook for 2-3 minutes per side, or until the shrimp are pink and cooked through. Remove from heat and let cool slightly.
2. Make the Cocktail Sauce:
   - In a small bowl, combine ketchup, prepared horseradish, lemon juice, Worcestershire sauce, and hot sauce (if using). Adjust the amount of horseradish and hot sauce to your taste preference.
3. Chill the Shrimp:
   - Once cooked shrimp have cooled slightly, transfer them to a plate or bowl and refrigerate until chilled, about 30 minutes.
4. Assemble the Cajun Shrimp Cocktail:
   - Arrange the chilled Cajun shrimp on a serving platter or individual cocktail glasses.
   - Serve the shrimp with cocktail sauce on the side for dipping.

5. Garnish and Serve:
    - Garnish the Cajun shrimp cocktail with lemon wedges and chopped fresh parsley or cilantro, if desired.
    - Serve immediately as a flavorful and spicy appetizer.

This Cajun shrimp cocktail is a fantastic appetizer for parties or gatherings, offering a zesty and bold twist on the traditional shrimp cocktail. Adjust the amount of Cajun seasoning and hot sauce to suit your taste preferences for spice level. Enjoy the succulent shrimp with the tangy cocktail sauce for a delightful flavor experience!

Miniature Crab Cakes

Ingredients:

- 1 pound lump crabmeat, drained and picked over for shells

- 1/2 cup breadcrumbs (preferably panko)
- 1/4 cup mayonnaise
- 1 large egg, beaten
- 1 tablespoon Dijon mustard
- 2 tablespoons chopped fresh parsley
- 1 green onion, finely chopped
- 1/2 teaspoon Old Bay seasoning (or more to taste)
- Salt and pepper, to taste
- 1/4 cup vegetable oil, for frying

For the Remoulade Sauce:

- 1/2 cup mayonnaise
- 1 tablespoon Dijon mustard
- 1 tablespoon capers, drained and chopped
- 1 tablespoon chopped fresh parsley
- 1 tablespoon chopped green onion
- 1 tablespoon lemon juice
- 1 teaspoon Worcestershire sauce
- Salt and pepper, to taste

Instructions:

1. Prepare the Crab Cakes:
    - In a large mixing bowl, combine the lump crabmeat, breadcrumbs, mayonnaise, beaten egg, Dijon mustard, chopped parsley, green onion, Old Bay seasoning, salt, and pepper. Gently mix until well combined, being careful not to break up the crabmeat too much.
2. Form the Miniature Crab Cakes:
    - Scoop about 1-2 tablespoons of the crab mixture and form it into small patties or balls, depending on your preference.
    - Place the formed crab cakes on a baking sheet lined with parchment paper. Chill in the refrigerator for at least 30 minutes to help them firm up.
3. Cook the Crab Cakes:
    - Heat vegetable oil in a large skillet over medium heat.
    - Carefully place the chilled crab cakes in the skillet, working in batches if necessary to avoid overcrowding. Cook for 3-4 minutes on each side, or until golden brown and heated through. Use a spatula to gently flip the crab cakes halfway through cooking.
    - Transfer the cooked crab cakes to a plate lined with paper towels to absorb any excess oil. Keep warm while you prepare the remoulade sauce.
4. Make the Remoulade Sauce:

- In a small bowl, combine mayonnaise, Dijon mustard, chopped capers, chopped parsley, chopped green onion, lemon juice, Worcestershire sauce, salt, and pepper. Mix well until smooth and creamy.
5. Serve:
    - Arrange the miniature crab cakes on a serving platter.
    - Serve warm, with the remoulade sauce on the side for dipping or drizzling over the crab cakes.
6. Enjoy:
    - Garnish with additional chopped parsley or green onion if desired, and serve immediately as a delicious appetizer.

These miniature crab cakes are flavorful and crispy on the outside, with tender and juicy crabmeat on the inside. The creamy remoulade sauce adds a tangy and zesty complement to the sweetness of the crab. They are sure to be a hit at any party or gathering, offering a taste of gourmet seafood in a bite-sized form!

www.ingramcontent.com/pod-product-compliance
Lightning Source LLC
LaVergne TN
LVHW062048070526
838201LV00080B/2201